RUGBY SKILLS
TACTICS
AND RULES
REVISED & UPDATED

RUGBY SKILLS
TACTICS
AND RULES
REVISED & UPDATED

TONY WILLIAMS & FRANK BUNCE

First published in the UK in 2008 by
A & C Black Publishers Ltd
36 Soho Square
London W1D 3QY
www.acblack.com

Reprinted 2010

First published in New Zealand in 2008 by
David Bateman Ltd,
30 Tarndale Grove
Albany, Auckland

ISBN: 978-1-408-10914-4

Note: Whilst every effort has been made to ensure that the content of this book is technically
accurate and as sound as possible, neither the authors nor the publishers can accept responsibility
for any injury or loss sustained as a result of use of this material.

Design and typesetting: Jag Creative
Photographs: Photosport
Printed in China through Colorcraft Ltd, Hong Kong

CONTENTS

3. BASIC SKILLS: PASSING   38

4. BASIC SKILLS: CATCHING   48

7. SPECIALIZED SKILLS 70

8. SET PLAY: THE SCRUM 84

also being trialled in South Africa throughout that season. These variations were designed to make play more fluid and create a faster, more exciting game that would also be more easily understood. At the time it was expected that if any of them were to be adopted permanently, they would come into operation towards the end of 2009. As a result of the trials, in May 2009, the International Rugby Board (IRB) Council agreed to make some amendments to the laws. These came into effect from 23 May of that year.

The sections of the laws mainly affected are:
- Law 6: Match officials
- Law 19: Touch and the line out — Who gets the throw-in? and Line-out laws
- Law 20: Scrum — Offside at the scrum
- Law 22: In-goal — Ball dead in-goal

These changes have now been incorporated into the relevant laws in chapter 16, pages 140–157.

While the trials initiated in 2008 have now been completed, there is a possibility that the IRB may undertake further trials on other aspects of the laws in the future. See the IRB website at www.irb.com for the most up-to-date information and specific details on all current rugby rules and laws.

ACKNOWLEDGEMENTS

Many thanks to the editorial staff who have worked so hard in the background to produce this book, and to Gordon Hunter, former All Blacks selector, sadly now deceased, who contributed so much to the coaching section in the previous edition of this book.

AUTHORS' NOTE:
EXPERIMENTAL LAW VARIATIONS

In 2008, when this book first went to press, a number of experimental law variations (ELVs) were being trialled in the Super 14 competition for that year between teams from New Zealand, Australia and South Africa, with the full set of ELVs

INTRODUCTION

THE GAME FOR ALL

One of the most exciting rugby players in the world at the moment is All Black Dan Carter. When Dan was a boy his parents got fed up with him kicking the rugby ball on to their roof, so they built him a set of rugby posts at the bottom of the yard, and there he would practise hour after hour.

As talented as Dan Carter is, it is learning the techniques and practising them over and over that made him a skilled rugby player. (A technique is simply a way of doing something that works.) How these techniques are put to use in a team situation is called tactics. But that's not enough: you also have to know the laws. Rugby is a simple game, but the laws can be complex. The key to success and enjoyment in rugby is to master the skills, know the laws and use the best tactics for the situation.

Rugby Skills, Tactics and Rules simplifies the game so that a child of about 10 can understand it, but it also offers a broader knowledge for more

One of the most complete players in the world — All Blacks captain Richie McCaw.

experienced players and coaches. It begins with an explanation of the individual skills — from the most basic through to the specialized — followed by unit and team skills, moves and strategies, each layered one on top of the other. Towards the back of the book is a plain-language guide to the laws of rugby and a glossary, so that rugby terms can be clearly understood. Every time you struggle to understand, make a long kick to the glossary and clear up the meaning of that unfamiliar rugby term!

Read this book, reread it, watch, learn and practise. Rugby is the game with the most laws because it actually has the most freedoms. It allows you to express yourself in so many ways, such as kicking and passing the ball, tackling, pushing, pulling and getting muddy. Unlike most sports, you can use every part of your body, and there is no feeling in the world like running with the ball in open space, the opposition chasing after you, the goal line getting closer and closer.

Rugby Skills, Tactics and Rules gives you the basis of how to play rugby. After that it is up to players and coaches to be innovative and come up with new tricks and moves and, above all, to have fun!

TOP: The thrilling sight of South African winger Bryan Habana in full flight.

BOTTOM: Drew Mitchell of Australia, with ball in hand, is an exciting newcomer to rugby.

13

1. THE TEAM

RUGBY IS A TEAM SPORT

The objective in rugby is to score more points than your opponents. This can be achieved by scoring tries (the rugby equivalent of American football's touchdowns), kicking goals or a combination of both.

Scoring tries is the real joy of rugby. Though individuals score tries, rugby is a team sport, and every member of the team contributes in some way to the tries that are scored.

The team that takes the field consists of 15 people, but up to seven "extra" players can sit on the bench and be used as replacements during the game. These extra players are generally known as substitutes or reserves. Sometimes the rugby 15 is written in Roman numerals — XV (X for 10 and V for 5).

England's scrum is low, determined and ready to engage.

- The ball cannot be passed or thrown forward.
- The most important law in rugby is "advantage", which keeps the game continuous.

FORWARDS AND BACKS

In the very early days of rugby, the game was played with a pig's bladder and, in Europe, sometimes contested by whole villages. Some players would go forward to join the huge mass of bodies wrestling for the "ball", while others would stay back, ready to have a run with it when it came free. In this way the two basic positions in rugby, forwards and backs, were formed. Forwards go forward to win the ball; backs stay back to run with it.

Nowadays a rugby team consists of eight forwards and seven backs. The forwards are usually subdivided into the front row (three), the second row (two) and the back row (three). The backs are referred to as the halves (two), the three-quarters (four) and the fullback (one).

THE KEY RUGBY LAWS

Rugby laws are covered later in the book, but here are the most important ones, which you should know from the beginning:

- Any player can do anything, except only front row players can play in the front row.
- Rugby is a game played on the feet.

Sébastien Chabal of France (known as the Caveman) concentrates on the simplest skill of all — catching the ball.

THE BASICS

Every player in a team has similar individual skills, such as passing and catching. The level of the passing skills should be high throughout the team, no matter what the position.

The team itself has unit skills, such as the front row of the scrum that pushes as a unit. There are forward skills, such as are required in scrums and line outs, and back skills, such as speed and deception. Then there are team skills in which different units or individuals work with other units or individuals.

THE POSITIONS

The position in a rugby team tells a player where they are to stand on the field, how to fit into a team and what their duties are. The names given to the 15 different positions have changed over the years, with regional variations also confusing the issue. In New Zealand, for example, the names given to the backs are based on a system determined by their distance from the scrum: halves, five-eighths, centre, three-quarters and fullback. In other parts of the world the halfback is usually called the scrum half; the first five-eighth is known as the fly half, outside half or stand off; the centres are the inside centre and the outside centre and so on.

The first two rows of the scrum, the front row and the second row, are together called the tight five because they do most of the hard work, trying to win the ball in close situations such as scrums, line outs, rucks and mauls. In the third row there are two flankers, one on each side of the scrum, and the number eight is in between them, at the back of the scrum. These players are also called

Romanian second row forward Cristian Petre bends low to act as scrum half. Any player can do anything on a rugby field (but only front row forwards can play in the front row).

The basic positions of a rugby team. The forwards are close to the ball. The backs are spread out ready to run with the ball or to defend against an attack.

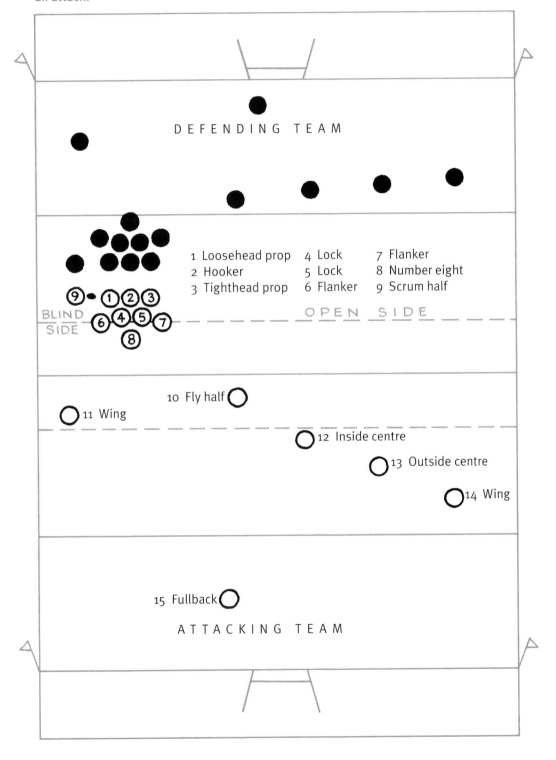

DEFENDING TEAM

1 Loosehead prop	4 Lock	7 Flanker
2 Hooker	5 Lock	8 Number eight
3 Tighthead prop	6 Flanker	9 Scrum half

BLIND SIDE

OPEN SIDE

10 Fly half

11 Wing

12 Inside centre

13 Outside centre

14 Wing

15 Fullback

ATTACKING TEAM

loose forwards, or loosies, because they do more running in order to get to the ball first. For the sake of consistency this book will use the terms that are generally understood throughout most of the rugby-playing world. These terms are shown in the diagram on the previous page.

POSITIONS WITH ALTERNATIVE NAMES

- Prop
- Hooker
- Second row or lock
- Flanker, wing forward or loosie
- Number eight (also referred to as a loosie)
- Scrum half or halfback
- Fly half, first five-eighth or pivot
- Inside centre or second five-eighth
- Centre
- Wing or wing three-quarter
- Fullback

PROP

The word prop means "to hold up or support", and that is what props do. (In France a prop is called a *pilier* — a pillar.) The props support the hooker in a set scrum or a jumper at the line out and at kick restarts. A prop needs strength and good technique.

There are two props — the loosehead prop (who wears the number one jersey) and the tighthead prop (number three jersey). In rugby, jerseys are numbered from left to right. The loosehead stands on the left side of the hooker, the side where the scrum half puts the ball into the scrum. They are called loosehead props because

HOW TO PICK AN AGE-GROUP TEAM BASED ON BASIC SKILLS

Prop — the two most solidly built players (not fast runners)

Hooker — solidly built and a good line-out thrower

Locks or Second row — the two tallest

Flankers — fittest of the forwards

Number eight — forward who is big, fit and skilful

Scrum half — best long passer

Fly half — best kicker and tactician

Centres — best tacklers and passers

Wings — the two fastest runners

Fullback — best catcher of the high ball

when the scrum binds, theirs is the "loose" (free) head on the outside of the scrum.

The loosehead's job is to make sure the hooker can get a good view of the ball when it is put in by the scrum half. To do this the loosehead has to be able to keep the opposing prop from disrupting the scrum and obstructing the hooker's view.

The tighthead prop stands on the other side of the hooker. The tighthead's job is to keep the scrum firm and steady on the team's put-in and to try to disrupt it when the opposition is putting the ball in. Ideally, because of the dynamics (energies and pressures) of the scrum, the tighthead prop

The front row consists of three strong players —
two props with a hooker in between.

TOP: A ruck — players are off their feet and the ball is on the ground. The South African players (green) are not allowed to pick it up and must drive through the ruck to try and win it. The Argentinean players (on their feet) can pick it up as soon as it has come out on their side of the ruck.

BOTTOM: A maul — the ball is held in the hand and players contesting for it must stay on their feet.

RUCK AND MAUL DEFINITIONS

Ruck — a ruck occurs when one or more players from each team try to push their opponents off the ball when it is on the ground.

Maul — a maul occurs when at least three players (the player with the ball and one more from each team) try to wrestle for the ball when it is being held in the hand.

Main skills — scrummaging, supporting taller players at kickoffs and line outs.

Main practice — strength training and scrummaging.

would be the tallest in the front row, followed by the hooker, and the loosehead prop should be the shortest.

Traditionally the props would stand at numbers one and three in the line out to support the main jumpers (usually the second rowers) who would stand at positions two and four. This is a good way to organize an age-group team, though in higher grades players at the line out move around a lot these days to try to trick the opposition. The props, or whoever is next to the jumper, must protect the jumper from interference, assist the jump and protect the ball from the other team. Because of their strength, props are often used to rip the ball free at mauls and to charge forward with the ball alongside rucks, mauls and line outs.

The Italian front row waits for the referee's signal before engaging with the waiting Australians.

One of the main skills of a hooker is throwing the ball accurately into a line out.

HOOKER

A hooker is a prop with specialized tasks. The first task of hookers is to use their feet to "hook" the ball back in set scrums. Sometimes the team not putting in the ball wins the scrum and gains possession. The ball is supposed to be won by the team putting it in, who put it in from their loosehead side, so when the other team hooks it, it is called winning the ball "against the head" or getting a "tighthead".

These days, the hooker is usually the player who throws the ball in at a line out. They are also expected to be mobile, operating almost as flankers when the flankers are tied up in a ruck or maul. Some teams have also developed moves using the hooker as the extra player, wide of the ruck or maul, to create an overlap.

Main skills — hooking the ball in the scrum, throwing the ball into the line out.

Main practice — scrummaging and throwing the ball straight into the line out.

SECOND ROW

The two tallest people in the team are usually the second row forwards (or locks), whose main job is to win the ball at the line outs. They also provide the main forward thrust in the scrums. Second rows should be strong and tough; along with the front row, they are the tight forwards who are expected to do the hard work at the rucks, mauls and scrums. In the modern game, second rows are also expected to be mobile and good passers of the ball.

Main skills — catching the line-out ball, scrummaging.

Main practice — jumping for and catching a line-out ball, scrummaging.

Second row forward Bakkies Botha of South Africa
stretches to take a catch at the line out.

Richie McCaw of New Zealand carries out one of the main roles of the flanker — tackling.

NUMBER EIGHT

Number eights are key players at scrum time because they are able to link with the backs. They are the only forwards allowed to pick up the ball from the back of the scrum.

The number eight should have a good, almost telepathic, understanding with the scrum half. The combination between the number eight and the scrum half is vital to provide clean ball for the backs to set the attack with. The ideal number eight is a mix of all the forwards: big and tough but also intelligent and skillful. They must also be mobile and good tacklers.

Main skills — tackling, running with the ball in hand.

Main practice — tackling, linking with the scrum half.

FLANKER

The flankers operate from the sides of the scrum and leave it first, as their job is to get to the ball as quickly as possible. Some teams play with right and left flankers who always stay on their own sides of the scrum, but most teams play with open-side and blind-side flankers.

The scrum is set at the exact position where play breaks down. Usually there is a larger distance to the touch-line on one side of the scrum than on the other. The side with the greater distance is called the open side, and the side with the shorter distance is called the blind side.

Main skills — tackling, reading the play, fitness.
Main practice — tackling, running.

Scrum halves must be very good passers. They are the link between the forwards and the backs.

The open-side flanker should be one of the fittest players on the team. Their task is to be the first player to the ball when play breaks down. The breakdown is where play comes to a temporary stop when someone is tackled. Both sides then compete for the ball, but the laws concerning the breakdown are very strict.

Open-side flankers must know these laws well. They must also be skilled at getting back to their feet after they have made the tackle so they can legitimately try to win the ball. (Laws 14 and 15 on pages 148–149 cover the breakdown.)

Open-side flankers should also have the explosive speed of a back. At training they should practise with the backs often in order to improve their speed and ball-handling skills. Knowing the backs' moves can help the flanker arrive at the breakdown area first.

Blind-side flankers are more of a cross between a second row forward and an open-side flanker. They should be fit and fast, as well as tall and strong. Their additional size and strength is required for blind-side defence, and their height increases the options at the back of the line out. Both flankers must be excellent tacklers.

SCRUM HALF

Scrum halves are often the smallest player on the team, as they have to bend low to retrieve the ball from the back of the scrum or ruck. They are the link between the backs and the forwards.

Main skills — passing, decision making.
Main practice — long passing off either hand, kicking.

The fly half must be a skilled kicker. Jonny Wilkinson of England is one of the best.

Passing is the key skill of scrum halves. Their passes must be fast, long and accurate, and they should be able to pass equally well off either hand.

Scrum halves must be quick thinkers, frequently having to decide whether to leave the ball with the forwards, pass to the backs, go left or right, kick or run with it themselves. They should run with the ball themselves when they sense an opening close to the scrum, ruck or breakdown. The best scrum halves have a fast turn of speed from a standing start.

Scrum halves should be confident and communicative. They have to tell their forwards when and how they want the ball and order them around if necessary. Both the scrum half and the fly half must realize that it is their job to control the game to their team's advantage.

FLY HALF

The fly half is the key position on the rugby field. Scrum halves control play close to the forwards, which means they are often too close to the play to see it as well as they would like, and they are always under pressure from the opposition forwards. Standing further back and protected by the long pass of their scrum half, fly halves have the luxury of a little more time and space, so they are in a better position to read the game and decide the best tactics. The extra time usually allows them to kick or pass before the opposition defence can get to them.

They should be able to kick accurately with either foot and preferably also kick long distances. Because fly halves are usually less muscled than other players, they are often light on their feet, able to break the defensive line with little side steps, jinks and darts. Then they usually link up with the faster runners outside them.

CENTRE

There are two centres. These days most teams play an inside centre and an outside centre. The inside centre is always closer to the scrum or line out (in New Zealand the inside centre is called a second five-eighth). It is also possible to play left and right centres, with both players keeping their position, even if the scrum is on the left or right of the field. When the ball is won and passed to the backs, the point at which the tackle is made is usually in midfield. Therefore, the centres must be strongly built and excellent tacklers.

The inside centre is usually more skillful, similar to a fly half, and should be skilled at creating doubt in the minds of the opposition. In the modern game, the inside centre is often used as a "battering ram" to set up the next phase of the attack. Outside centres tend to be more strongly built, but they should also be skilled at setting up plays, particularly to the wing outside them. They should be very good at passing the ball, especially with the timing of the pass.

Main skills — kicking, passing.
Main practice — kicking, especially punting, tactics.

Main skills — tackling, passing.
Main practice — tackling, timing a pass.

WING

The wings should be the fastest players on the team. Their main jobs are to score tries and chase kicks.

Main skills — speed and elusiveness.
Main practice — sprint practice.

One of the key skills of a centre, in this case former All Blacks captain Tana Umaga, is timing when to give the pass.

FULLBACK

A fullback should be able to tackle like a centre, have the speed of a wing and possess the kicking skills of a fly half. They should be good at catching a high ball, especially under pressure. In the early days of rugby, the role of the fullback was almost completely defensive. Today, fullbacks are important attacking weapons, entering the back line to create an "extra player" for their team. Timing their entry into the line is an important skill.

Main skills — catching a high ball, tackling, defensive cover, timing the entry into the line.
Main practice — catching a high ball and kicking it either up field or into touch.

The fullback has to be very good at catching the high ball.

RUNNING

There are five basic rugby skills that every player should possess. They are running, passing, catching, tackling and attitude. These are the foundations of all team play.

A foot race for the ball between England hooker Mark Regan (left) and French centre David Marty (right).

Running is the most basic of all rugby skills: being fit enough to chase the kick ahead, supporting one's own players with the ball or getting back in defence to make a tackle will often decide which team wins the game.

KEY RUNNING SKILLS
RUN STRAIGHT

Unless attempting to evade an individual tackler, players should run straight. Imagine the rugby field to be made up of lanes: don't run in someone else's lane, otherwise the attack will drift sideways and run out of space near the sidelines. Running straight draws in the defenders and leaves space on the outside in which to make an attack.

RUN TOWARDS SUPPORT

Ball carriers should always be aware of their
support players. If they spot a gap they should
take it. When they have a choice, they should take
the option that makes it easy for their support to
get to them.

As Andy Ellis breaks away,
he has two fellow All Blacks
in close support.

Support play is essential to keep the attack moving forward.

SUPPORT PLAY

Support players should always try to position themselves where they can receive a pass. When there are several players in support, they should spread out on either side of the ball carrier and attack in an arrowhead formation. Support players should follow a forward closely in order to take a short pass or join the ruck or maul that may form.

Support play wins matches. Players should be fit enough to keep up with the play. An attack only breaks down when it runs out of support, and a try is only scored when the opposition runs out of defence options.

RUNNING AFTER THE BALL

In the past, the general law in defence was that forwards chase the ball to the next ruck or maul. In modern rugby, forwards are expected to read the game and make their own decisions as to what is needed. Often they will stand out from the breakdown, waiting to stop the next attack. Backs usually maintain their defensive positions, marking the player opposite them. Players should also learn to "read" the play so they can arrive at a point on the field at the same time as the ball. Rather than run to where the ball is, they should run to where they think the ball will be by the time they get there. This is especially true of flankers, and also wingers, who may have to run from the other side of the field to make a covering tackle.

CARRYING THE BALL

The ball can be carried in one or both hands. What is important is that the carrier be able to pass it quickly if needed.

Players can run faster with the ball in one hand, but they have more options available and a better chance of deceiving their opponents when they run with the ball in two hands, as their opponents cannot be sure if they are going to kick it or pass it. With the ball in one hand a player is clearly going to run.

When being held in one hand, the ball should be tucked tight against the chest. Some players have hands big enough to grasp it securely with only one hand, but this is not recommended, as the ball can be lost easily.

The ball should always be held in the hand that's farthest away from the nearest opponent. If an opponent approaches more closely from the other side, the ball should be transferred to the other hand. This protects the ball from the opposition.

THE FORWARD CHARGE

The player charging forward runs at full speed straight at an opponent. The ball is held firmly and hugged tightly against the chest so that it won't be knocked loose at the moment of impact. When this player is two or three paces away from the opposition player about to tackle them, they lower a shoulder and aim it at the tackler, trying to knock them out of the way. If the tackler is beaten, the player continues on to the next tackler.

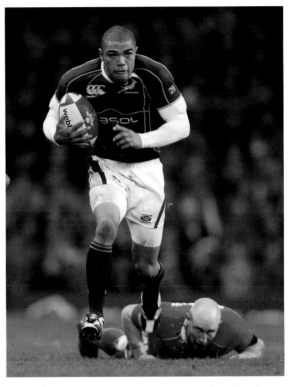

Bryan Habana carries the ball in one hand so he can run faster, but he will soon hold it in two to pass to J.P. Pietersen, so Pieterson can score.

Imanol Harinordoquy of France makes a forward charge against a strong English defence.

33

Nathan Sharpe of Australia on a forward charge. He will drive straight ahead, trying to suck in opposition defenders.

For an effective fend, the arm must be straightened at the point of impact to push off the tackler.

THE FEND OFF OR HANDOFF

The attacker runs straight at the tackler, the ball safely tucked up in the arm farthest from the tackler. As the attacker gets almost within touching distance, they reach out with the nearest arm, which is bent, and straighten it immediately at the moment of contact, pushing the tackler away and, at the same time, pushing themselves off the tackler. The attacker then has to accelerate away before the tackler recovers.

THE HIT AND SPIN

This is a forward charge in which the attacking player, instead of making full impact with the tackler, spins out of the tackle and keeps running (or spins around to pass the ball to a teammate). The attacker's shoulder is dropped into the lower body of the defender. The attacker then drives to the side where their body overlaps that of the defender, twisting the hips, taking small steps and spinning out of the tackle.

His arm extended in a fend, Cédric Heymans of France leans away to try to get out of the tackle.

THE BUMP

The bump is a version of the forward charge and is especially useful if the tackler is set low. As the attacker comes into the tackle, they suddenly lower their body and give the tackler a shove with the shoulder. This cannot be done if the tackler is set high for the tackle.

DECEPTIVE RUNNING

The ball carrier will often use deception and balance to beat a tackler. Deception relies on making the tackler think twice, causing hesitation. Balance is a matter of being light on the feet and trying to cause the would-be tackler to be heavy footed. There are several versions of deceptive running.

THE SWERVE

The attacker runs straight at the tackler but about three or so paces away starts to curve away, still running fast, and passes beyond the tackler's reach.

OUTSIDE CUT

The outside cut is also known as an "in-and-out". It is like a swerve except the lines taken are straighter, and it is usually done near the touch-line. The attacker runs away from the defender then cuts back towards them, making them stop or hesitate. The attacker then changes the angle sharply to the outside again and sprints away.

THE SIDE STEP

The attacking player gets as close as possible to the tackler without being in the tackler's reach

Alun Wyn Jones of Wales steps around Aleki Lutui of the Pacific Islands.

then slows suddenly by taking a short step. This will cause the attacker to automatically drop a shoulder in the direction of the short step and thrust with the opposite leg, effectively moving sideways at speed. As soon as the attacker has stepped to the side of the tackler, they must straighten up and accelerate to get clear.

DODGE OR DART

A very sudden change of direction to the left or right, angled away from the tackler. Like the feint (see following page), the shoulder leans towards the defender before short, rapid steps take the attacking player beyond the tackler's reach.

Drew Mitchell of Australia uses pace and evasion to score against Japan.

THE PROP

A version of the side step in which only a small step is taken, immediately followed by a hard push off one leg to get past the tackler.

THE FEINT

The attacker drops a shoulder to suggest they are going to run one way, but they then go in a different direction, thereby deceiving the tackler.

Ruan Pienaar of South Africa sends England's Mike Brown off balance and steps outside him.

The England tackler has his feet planted, which makes it easier for Henry Tuilagi of Samoa to run around him.

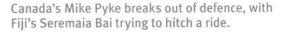
Canada's Mike Pyke breaks out of defence, with Fiji's Seremaia Bai trying to hitch a ride.

THE GOOSE STEP

Two or three quick steps in which the legs are lifted up with the knees locked. It suggests to the defender that a change of pace or direction is about to occur, causing hesitation. The goose step is useful only for deception; it does not add speed or movement.

THE FULL STOP

The full stop is when the attacker comes to a sudden stop, confusing the defender, who is likely to stop also. Then the attacker takes off again and will gain an advantage if the defender is slow to start up again.

Mahonri Schwalger of Samoa evades the tackle of England's Paul Sackey.

PASSING

Passing is the major skill in rugby. This is partly because the law that makes rugby unique is the one that says the ball cannot be passed forward. It can only be passed in a line level with the receiver or behind that line. Usually the ball is passed back, because to pass the ball level is to risk the referee calling it forward.

PASSING THEORY

Both teams start with 15 players, but positions on the field constantly change. The objective is to cause a situation in which the attacking players outnumber the defensive players. If they pass correctly, attackers will create what is called "an overlap" — an extra player who is unopposed and has the best chance of scoring.

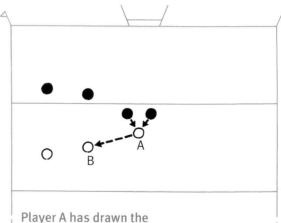

Player A has drawn the opposition defence and now passes to teammate B who is in a better position.

WHEN TO PASS

The ball is passed to a teammate who is in a better position, as shown in the diagram to the left. A player in a "better position" means one who is less likely to get tackled and has more room to move. In this case, player A passes the ball to another teammate (player B) who is in a better position, and if this is continued, sooner or later one of the players will be in the best position of all — the position to score a try.

As an opposing player comes within tackling distance, All Black Ma'a Nonu passes the ball out of his reach to a teammate.

HOSPITAL PASS

A player should not pass to a teammate who is in a worse position. The most extreme example of this is known as the "hospital pass" as the player could potentially be injured as a result. If a player receives the ball just as a tackler arrives, their eye will be focused on the ball in order to catch it, not on the tackler, so a collision could happen. In this case, the player who passed the ball should have held on to it instead of passing.

PASSING TECHNIQUE

The whole body is used when passing the ball (except for some variations described later). The player holds the ball in two hands, then, like drawing back a golf club, the arms first swing the opposite way before they swing back again in the direction of the pass. The feet should be placed so the body is well balanced to allow a slight sway of the hips. This all helps to give the ball direction and speed. After the pass has been made, the player will automatically recoil slightly in the opposite direction. If the player is running, there should be no break in the stride when making the pass.

AIMING THE PASS

Some younger players think that passing simply means getting rid of the ball before they are tackled. A pass should be more like giving a present. Passers direct the ball to receivers and make it as easy as possible for them to catch it. The ball should arrive in front of the chest so that they can easily reach out with their hands to catch it. This means catchers are also able to keep their heads up (a low pass will force them to look down and be less aware of the

Argentinean fullback Juan Martin Hernandez is perfectly poised to deliver a pass.

play around them). If receivers are running, the ball must be thrown in front of them so they can run to it and catch it without breaking stride.

TIMING THE PASS

The timing of the pass is critical. The defence is trying to predict when the pass will come, and it is the ball carrier's job to deceive them. If the receiver is in a lot of space, the pass might go early to allow this teammate to take advantage of it. Sometimes the passer will leave the pass as late as possible in order to draw a defender (see below). The exact timing of the pass is a matter of judgement, and in each situation passers must follow their instinct.

PASSING ON

Passing on means to shift the ball out wide. The player receiving the ball passes it as soon as it is received.

DRAWING THE PLAYER

When the ball carrier is marked by a defender and the likely receiver is unmarked, the ball carrier draws the defender, delaying the pass until the last possible moment. If the carrier were to pass the ball right away, the defender would have time to change direction and tackle the new ball carrier. So the ball carrier draws (attracts) the defender by running straight at them as if to take the tackle. Just before the defender makes the tackle, the ball carrier passes the ball to the teammate, at which point it's too late for the defender to change direction. Ideally, the defender is so committed to the tackle that they actually make contact with the passer, but too late — the ball is gone.

Anthony Tuitavake of the Auckland Blues holds the ball to his left (TOP), ready to pass it to his right. He then swings his arms to his right and releases the ball (BOTTOM).

Heini Adams halfway through a dive pass. His arms will thrust out and throw the ball.

Augustin Pichot of Argentina releases the pass. His right arm has crossed over his left arm, showing that it was probably a spin pass.

French scrum half Pierre Mignoni has his feet planted wide with his body leaning forward, and he is coiled, ready to spin out a pass in one smooth action.

DELAYING THE PASS

Sometimes an advantage is gained by holding on to the ball a little longer, either to fool the defence or to allow time for a teammate to come through at speed (while the defence is standing still). The delayed pass gives the receiving player the time and space to break the line. This is a great skill that, when done well, is very hard to defend against.

DIFFERENT TYPES OF PASSES

SPIN OR SPIRAL PASS

In this pass, the hand that is opposite to the direction of the pass comes up over the ball as the pass is thrown, causing the ball to spin. A spinning ball travels quicker than a non-spinning ball.

SCRUM-HALF PASS

This specialist pass by the scrum half clears the ball from the forwards out to the backs. It must be done quickly, before the opposition defence pours through, and in a single movement from first touch of the ball to its release.

While awaiting delivery of the ball, the scrum half must be set "cocked like a gun", ready to fire the ball immediately. The passer does not glance at the receiver while waiting for the ball because this alerts the defenders that the ball is coming out.

If passing left, the scrum half's right foot is nearest to the ball. The other foot is positioned about a hip's width away, pointing towards the receiver. The knees are slightly bent. The arms are extended so that as soon as the defender receives the ball, they swing both arms through a wide arc with the force of the whole body. It is vital that the pass is made in one motion. Precious time is lost if the scrum half has to wind up for the swing or take any steps. Most scrum halves also make the ball spin for greater speed and distance.

LONG PASS

Any pass that is thrown a long distance.

AMERICAN FOOTBALL PASS

Though not used often, the American football style of pass for throwing long has been used in rugby from time to time. The ball is held in one hand, pulled back over the shoulder and hurled like a spinning javelin. Of course, in rugby this pass cannot be thrown forward.

DIVE PASS

This is a quick pass used when the scrum half has not been able to get into the proper position for a long pass. The scrum half dives forward and throws the ball at the same time. The ball is gripped in both hands and thrown from below the waist, through the length of the upper body in a scooping

In this dive pass, Matt Giteau's arms are at full extension after he has released the ball.

motion and released when the passer's arms are fully stretched. After the pass, the scrum half will naturally end up on the ground. This is a very effective way of clearing the ball quickly when the scrum half is under pressure from the opposition.

REVERSE PASS

The reverse pass is a variation of the long pass in which scrum halves have their backs to the receiver. Usually scrum halves are forced into this position by receiving scrappy ball from the forwards. The passer throws the ball out of the back of the hand and behind the back, with the hand coming over the ball to create spin. However, the scrum half is virtually throwing blind and has to be aware of the position of the receiver. This pass is seen less often these days. It is a great skill and looks spectacular, but it is not that hard to learn.

LOB PASS

The lob pass is a deliberate, high-looping toss of the ball that takes it over the heads of defenders to a teammate.

POP PASS

The pop pass is a very short pass: the ball is simply "popped up" in a small loop (usually no more than about an arm's length) to a player who is coming through at speed.

George Gregan of Australia looks set to give a short pop pass to his teammate who is coming in close.

UNUSUAL PASSES

There are a variety of passes that can be used in special situations. In many of these cases, the ball is passed using only the arms and hands — without the force and weight of the body — and sometimes just the hands.

FLICK PASS

The flick pass is a short pass thrown quickly with a flick of the wrist.

FAST PASS

The fast pass is used when the player receiving the ball is about to be tackled. The ball is treated like a hot potato: the moment it touches the hands, it is flicked straight on to a teammate.

THE OFFLOAD

The offload is a pass used when players "offload" (unload or pass the ball) as they are being tackled or right after they have been tackled. This is an improvised pass; the player just gets the ball to a teammate any way possible.

ONE-HANDED PASS

The one-handed pass is used when a player is unable to use both hands, for example, when being tackled.

OVERHEAD PASS

With the overhead pass, the ball is lobbed with one hand over a defender's head to a teammate.

Jacques Fourie of South Africa flips the pass out of the back of his hand as he is tackled.

Hare Makiri (right) about to offload the ball to Koji Taira (left), who scores.

South Africa's Jacques Fourie has a leg, but the USA player's arms are free, and he will get his pass away if he has a player in support.

New Zealand Sevens player Edwin Cocker offloads in the tackle to Josh Blackie.

BASKETBALL PASS

The basketball pass is one in which the ball is thrown with two hands over a defender's head to a teammate.

THE REVERSE FLICK

A player running forward knows — or gets a call — that a teammate is following behind. Without looking, the passer flicks the ball back to that teammate out of the back of the hand. When successful, this pass can be devastating because no one expects it, and it can change the direction of the attack.

CHANGE-OF-DIRECTION PASS

The change-of-direction pass is intended to deceive. The ball carrier is about to pass the ball one way but instead holds on to it, twists around and passes it another way.

THE "ANYTHING GOES" PASS

The whole purpose of passing is to get the ball into the hands of a teammate who is in a better position. In tackled-ball situations or crowded traffic, players might invent all sorts of ways of passing the ball. If they get the ball into the hands of a teammate who is in a better position than themselves, no matter how untidy or unusual the pass might appear, it is a good pass.

Despite a heavy tackle from Owen Lentz of the USA, Kane Thompson of Samoa gets his pass away.

DECEPTIVE PASSES

The following are some of the many ways of deceiving members of the opposing team by not passing the ball.

THE DUMMY PASS

The ball carrier goes through all the motions of passing the ball, but at the moment of release holds on to it and darts through a gap. The trick to "throwing a dummy" is that if the ball carriers themselves believe they are going to pass the ball, so will the defenders.

THE DUMMY KICK

Similar to the dummy pass, the ball carrier pretends to be about to kick. When the tackler hesitates, the carrier makes for a gap, ball still in hand.

THE NON-PASS

A version of the dummy pass. The ball carrier is running at speed with the ball in one hand then, clasping it with both hands, slows slightly as if about to pass and suddenly takes off again.

DECOYS

Decoys are players who run as though they are going to take a pass. Decoys are very useful for confusing the opposition's defence.

By running with the ball in two hands Mauro Bergamasco of Italy will keep the opposition guessing. He can run, kick or pass on either side.

CATCHING

As soon as the ball is passed, it becomes the responsibility of the receiver to catch it. If the receiver fails to catch it cleanly and the ball is lost forward in the attempt, it is called a knock-on.

The referee may allow play to continue if the opposing side gains an advantage because of the knock-on, but the referee will stop play and award a scrum with the put-in given to the opposing side if there's no advantage. If, however, a player charges down a kick from an opponent, even if the ball hits the arms or hands, it is not ruled as a knock-on.

KEY CATCHING SKILLS

TO CATCH OR NOT TO CATCH

Receivers must first decide if they want to catch the ball. The pass might be so bad and the ball so far out of reach that the receiver may think it

All Black Jerry Collins is in the perfect position to take this pass, and his whole body is opened up ready to receive it.

is better to leave the ball than risk a knock-on. But a player who elects to catch the ball must commit completely to catching it effectively. As with anything else, catching is a skill and can be perfected with practise.

CATCHING A PASS

Even before the pass is made, catchers need to make sure they are in a good position to receive it. They must let the ball carrier know they are there and expecting the ball. This can be done through eye contact, shouting or even by using body language to show they are prepared to receive the ball. Similarly, catchers should be able to read the passer's body language so they know when to expect the pass.

Catchers should be to one side of the ball carrier and be coming up from a deeper position at speed. They should also angle their run to put themselves in a better attacking position than the player who is passing the ball.

Catchers should keep their eye on the ball until it is firmly in their hands. Though they might be tempted to plan what they are going to do next or look at the opposition tacklers, the key to catching is simply to keep your eye on the ball. Then the arms reach out, fingers splayed to fasten on to the ball, which is then clasped to the chest for extra security. A mistake some players make is to catch the ball against their chest. This can result in the ball hitting the chest first and bouncing off. The correct technique is to catch the ball with the hands first and then pull it into the chest.

CATCHING BAD PASSES

Bad passes could end up behind the catcher, over their heads or around their toes. Catchers have to

Perfect concentration and technique from Ben Blair. His eye on the high ball, his arms and chest form a basket in which to catch it.

decide if they can catch the ball without risking a knock-on. This is entirely the catcher's decision. If the ball is close to their feet, catchers might try to stop it with their foot, like a soccer player. In some situations they might decide to hack it forward and chase it. If the ball is catchable, no matter how bad the pass, it is the receiver's job to catch it. To achieve this, players should practise catching bad passes in training by getting teammates to sling all sorts of terrible passes at them.

CATCHING A WET BALL

In wet weather, passes should be shorter and more care should be taken with accuracy. The catcher has to concentrate even harder. This type of catch can also be practised at training by soaking the ball in a bucket of water and dishwashing liquid.

Seru Rabeni of Fiji has his eye on the ball despite the pressure from Drew Mitchell of Australia, who must wait for Rabeni to land on the ground before he can make the tackle.

CATCHING FROM A KICK

When catching a high ball from a kick, catchers must keep their eye on the ball. If they do this they will automatically move towards the point where the ball will land. They must call loudly, indicating to their teammates nearby that they intend to catch the ball, and so avoiding a possible mix up or collision. Once they have positioned themselves underneath the ball, catchers should splay their fingers and hold their arms to make a "basket" with their chest. As the ball falls into it, they should immediately tighten their grip, pulling the ball into their chest.

If a player thinks an opponent might beat them to the ball, they can jump for it. No opposition player is allowed to tackle the catcher in the air, though they can challenge for the ball. At kick restarts, when opposition players are competing for the ball, forwards should be able to catch the ball cleanly above their heads.

CALLING A MARK

If players catch the ball within their own 22-metre area (22 metres is around 24 yards) from an opposition kick in open play, they can claim a mark (a fair catch) by shouting "mark". If the referee awards it, the player is given a free kick. However, catchers should play on until they hear the referee's whistle, as referees may not award the fair catch if, for example, they do not hear the player's shout.

NEVER LET A RUGBY BALL BOUNCE

A player should always try to catch a high ball kicked by an opposition player. The rule is you never let a rugby ball bounce — because of its odd

By deciding to jump, Lote Tuqiri of Australia is first to the ball.

Here both players jump, but Geordan Murphy of Ireland times his jump better and is able to claim the high ball.

Shane Horgan of Ireland jumps higher but looks too off balance to control the ball.

Will Gareth Thomas of Wales or Aurélien Rougerie of France claim this high ball?

shape you never know where it is going to bounce. Even young players who are unsure of their catching ability should always make a genuine attempt. Again, practice will perfect the skill.

CATCHING NEAR THE TOUCH-LINE

When players are attempting to catch the ball near the touch-line, they should be aware of where the line is. If possible, they should step outside the field of play so that both the ball and the line are in front of them. That also gives players the option of jumping, catching the ball in the air and landing in the field of play.

PICKING UP A BOBBING BALL

When the ball has been kicked along the ground, receivers must be careful to judge the uneven bounce so they do not knock it on when attempting to control it. If in any doubt, they should stop the ball with their foot and then pick it up.

PICKING UP THE BALL OFF THE GROUND

Players should also practise picking up a stationary ball off the ground at speed by running forward and scooping it up with one or both hands.

FALLING ON THE BALL

Falling on the ball is a great skill. It is usually done when the ball has gone loose behind the defensive line and opponents are charging through. The defending player runs back towards the team's own line, falls on the ball, gathers it up and springs back up in one fluid motion. If it is not possible to get up right away because, for example, the defender has to dive full length, at least the opposition will be temporarily stopped from gaining possession of the ball.

Jason Robinson of England is off balance, but has got underneath the ball and hugs it tightly to his chest.

Joe Worsley cleans up the loose ball on the ground for England.

TACKLING

Tackling is as basic to rugby as running. Full body contact is allowed, but without striking of any form or anything else that may be dangerous, such as grabbing above the shoulders.

A tackle comprises five elements — courage and judgement, timing, technique and, of course, the hit itself. With the correct technique, the smallest player can tackle the largest. Tackling is not a difficult skill to master, and it is very satisfying to execute the perfect tackle and dump your opponent on the turf.

The original meaning of the word "tackle" is to grab hold of the ropes that control the sails of a sailing ship. In rugby the idea is much the same — to grab hold of your opponent firmly enough so that you can control or restrict their progress. This can be achieved by putting them on the ground, by driving them back or by turning them around to face your team.

Tackling is very important to defensive patterns. General defensive pressure can also result in obtaining possession of the ball by forcing the opposition to make mistakes.

KEY TACKLING SKILLS
COURAGE AND JUDGEMENT

Courage in tackling is making the decision to tackle. Then the tackler must decide *how* to make the tackle. They must quickly judge the ball carrier's distance, speed and direction. Tacklers should not look at ball carriers' eyes or hands because they could be deceived by the body language. They should look at players' legs to judge whether they might step or swerve. Then they can decide what kind of tackle to make and where they will hit the ball carrier. The usual target area is between the knees and the chest. With practice and experience, a player will reach the stage where this will just flash through their mind so that making the right choice becomes instinctive.

Determined Romanian players drive back All Black
Nick Evans in the tackle.

Eliota Fuimaono-Sapolu of Samoa can find no way through a committed South African defence. Defence is about attitude.

Mike Pyke of Canada has gone too high; Drew Mitchell's body position is lower, and he might slip out of the tackle.

The Bergamascos, Mauro and Mirco of Italy, team up to gang tackle Ireland's Girvan Dempsey.

Bryan Habana leans into the midriff of an upright Paul Sackey, driving him backwards (TOP). As Habana continues the tackle, Sackey is carried off his feet and is driven to the ground (MIDDLE).

The French fullback seems to have read the situation and is poised to make the tackle.

TIMING

A key part of the tackle is closing the gap. Tacklers must choose the line of approach along which they are most likely to intercept the ball carrier and make the tackle. They have to decide the exact moment when the ball carrier is most vulnerable. Depending on the approach they take, they may force the ball carrier out of play or into the path of other players. This is called shepherding, the same way a shepherd controls the movement of sheep.

TECHNIQUE

The tackler must now commit fully to the tackle, leaning into the target area with the shoulder and thrusting with the legs. Ideally, tacklers drive the upper part of the ball carrier's body backwards while also wrapping up the ball carrier's legs or arms. Tacklers must use their arms in the tackle: a shoulder charge without using the arms is dangerous and will be penalized.

THE HIT

At this point, tacklers put all their weight into the impact, forcing the ball carrier backwards and down to the ground. The momentum of the attack is halted and, as sometimes happens, the ball may be knocked loose, giving the tackler's team the opportunity to gain possession.

THE FRONT-ON TACKLE

The most common tackle is the front-on tackle, in which the ball carrier runs straight at the tackler who faces them. In this case, tacklers lead with one shoulder and, for their own safety, place their head to one side of the ball carrier's body.

Bakkies Botha of South Africa is met front on by two Fijian players.

Note the low, driving body position of the English tackler who stops Australia's Stirling Mortlock in his tracks.

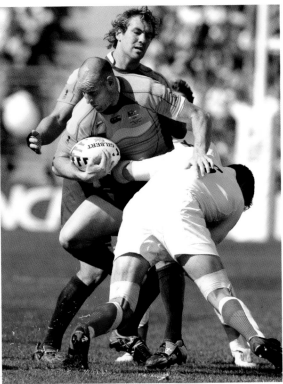

Ideally, the ball carrier becomes the victim of opposing forces: one force (the tackler's shoulder) pushes the upper body backwards, while the other force (the tackler's arms, which have dropped behind the knees) pull away the opponent's legs. The ball carrier is effectively being cut in half, with his upper body heading back while his lower body is pulled forward. The player's legs are no longer planted on the ground, so they have no strength (nothing to push off from) and no balance. The tackler is in complete control and can take the ball carrier to the ground.

THE END OF THE TACKLE

In the modern game, even when the hit has been made, the tackle is not over. The first part of a tackle is to stop the ball carrier; the second part is to try to gain possession of the ball. Now tacklers must get quickly to their feet and try to win the ball.

BODY POSITION

The key to effective tackling is good body position. At the moment of impact the tackler should be lower than the opposition and leaning towards them. If two people of the same weight are pushing against each other, then the one leaning into it more should win. The tackler has the advantage because the ball carrier, when running, will be relatively upright. At the moment of the hit, the tackler's back and legs should be straight, so that the whole body is pushing in one line, at an angle of about 35 degrees. In a well-timed tackle, the tackler launches forward and reaches the perfect angle at full extension just as the hit is made.

Mark Regan (number two) of England makes a side-on tackle of Berrick Barnes of Australia, which looks set to bring him to ground.

TACKLE PRACTICE

Practising with tackle bags is not sufficient because only one part of the tackle is being practised — the hit.

All the parts of the tackle described above should be practised until they can be done in one fluid motion.

Young rugby players can start by playing games of evasion in which they only have to touch their opponent to effect the tackle. Then elements of the tackle can be broken down and practised in slow motion — at walking pace, at a slow jog and so on. This should be done over and over again until every element becomes second nature.

As the players become familiar with these drills, the speed and difficulty can be increased by using (suitably padded) teammates as "tackle dummies". Tackling should be practised on both sides (left and right shoulders) and in a variety of situations.

TACKLING VARIATIONS AND TECHNIQUES
THE HALF HOLD

Sometimes in match situations tacklers are unable to complete the tackle, in which case they should at least hold on to the ball carrier and slow progress until they, or one of their own teammates, can finish off the tackle.

An Argentinean player chases down Frans Steyn of South Africa from behind.

SIDE-ON TACKLE

When tackling from the side, the shoulder is thrust into the ball carrier's hip. The arms go around the waist/hip area then slide down the attacker's thighs while the tackler maintains a firm hold. As the hold tightens, the ball carrier's legs will be pulled tighter together, causing the carrier to fall to the ground. The initial tackle can go higher — around the chest or waist — if attempting to stop the ball carrier from passing (see Smother Tackle on page 63).

TACKLE FROM BEHIND

This tackle is similar to the side-on tackle, except the tackler pursues the ball carrier who is taken from behind. Tacklers aim for the target area — the small of the back down to just below the buttocks — and envelop the waist or hips with their arms, sliding down the ball carrier's legs, bringing the run to an abrupt end.

THE ANKLE TAP

If unable to get close enough from behind to make the tackle, tacklers can reach out and strike the ankles of the ball carrier. They can dive forward and knock the ball carrier's nearest ankle against the other, tripping the carrier. The defender must then get up before the ball carrier and make an effort to complete the tackle.

STATIONARY TACKLE

If the tackler is stationary and the ball carrier is moving towards them at speed, the tackler can decide to just "accept" the tackle. The ball carrier will try to "run through" the tackler, so the tackler

should brace for the impact, get a firm hold and allow the ball carrier's momentum to take them both to the ground, rather like using the weight of an opponent in judo.

THE BIG HIT

The big hit usually happens when a player from the defending team is able to "read" the opposing team's pass and arrives just as an attacking player

BELOW: All Black Jerry Collins makes another big hit. Notice the low body position and how his whole body is driving into the tackle.

TOP RIGHT: Paul Emerick of the USA tackles Jason Robinson of England with a good low body position.

MIDDLE RIGHT: He drives through the tackle, knocking Robinson right off balance . . .

BOTTOM RIGHT: . . . and takes him to ground. Note how Emerick's hands are behind Robinson's knees. As Emerick's shoulder drove forward, his hands pulled Robinson's legs from under him.

This tackle is too high, is potentially dangerous and is likely to be penalized.

Jamie Robinson of Wales is tackled effectively, but his arms are still free to release the pass to Gavin Henson.

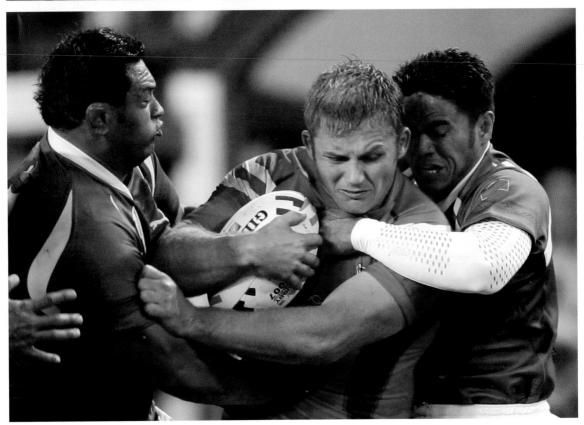

Owen Lentz of the USA is wrapped up by two of Samoa's players.

receives the ball. The attacker will be watching the ball, so the defender can smash the receiver backwards at the instant the pass is received. The big hit always looks spectacular.

SMOTHER TACKLE

In the smother tackle the defender's target is higher on the ball carrier's body, usually around the chest. There is less shoulder used and more emphasis on wrapping the arms around the attacker's arms so the ball cannot be passed to a teammate. The player executing the smother tackle is usually in a more upright position than normal.

DRIVING TACKLE

In a driving tackle, the attacker is upright and in a poor driving position, while the defender is leaning forward in a low driving position and pumping hard. Instead of being taken to the ground, in this case, the ball carrier can often be driven backwards several yards (or metres, which is the more common unit of measure for rugby), gaining an advantage for the defending team.

TOUCH-LINE TACKLING

When tackling close to the touch-line, the defending team should always try to drive the ball carrier over the touch-line to gain the throw-in to the line out. Prior to the tackle being made, the tackler should try to shepherd the ball carrier closer to the touch-line. At the moment of impact, the tackler completes the tackle with a rapid leg drive and a low body position. Alternatively, the tackled player can be pushed or dragged over the touch-line.

A perfect side-on tackle by South Africa's Jacques Fourie. His arms can now slide down the legs of Fiji's Kameli Ratuvou, stopping his run.

TURNING THE PLAYER IN THE TACKLE

In this tackle, the ball carrier has already been half tackled, and the tackler then twists the carrier so they are facing the defender's goal line. This makes it easier for the defending team's forwards to rip the ball from their opponent.

One of the most difficult and skilled tackles is being able to turn the ball carrier in the initial tackle. This is done by the tackler setting for a normal tackle, but instead of trying to knock the ball carrier back, allowing the carrier to partly come through, then spining in behind, holding the carrier just long enough for teammates to rip the ball away.

TACKLING A BIGGER PLAYER

Any player can tackle any other player on a rugby field no matter what their size. It is simply a matter of using the correct technique and ensuring that the ball carrier's legs are taken away so they cannot run.

DRAG-DOWN TACKLE

In the drag-down tackle, the ball carrier is standing upright and stationary, and tacklers wrap their arms around the body and drag the player to the ground, using the force of gravity.

GANG TACKLING

Two or more players are permitted to tackle the ball carrier at the same time. This is a good tactic in junior rugby when there is an opposing player who is especially big for the age group.

TACKLING THE FEND

When the ball carrier tries to fend off the tackler, the tackler has three options: go below the arm and use a powerful leg drive to break through the fend, grab the fending arm and use it in a half hold to get in closer and make a proper tackle, or hit the fend down and then make the tackle.

THE STRIP

Sometimes defenders are able to strip the ball from their opponent in the tackle. This is called "stripping the ball". They can also knock the ball loose with their shoulder.

ILLEGAL TACKLES

No player can tackle above the line of the shoulders (a head-high tackle) or pick up and throw or drop an opponent head first towards the ground (a spear tackle).

THE PERFECT TACKLE

Good tackling is mainly about technique, and a tackler should always try to execute each tackle with the best technique. However, players must remember that the main purpose of a tackle is to stop or slow the ball carrier in order to give the defenders the chance to win the ball.

A good tackle stops an attack, but a perfect tackle wins possession of the ball.

Smaller players can tackle big players. Here fly half Mike Hercus of the USA puts in a heavy tackle on giant English forward Simon Shaw.

The Canadian tackler has a good low body position but will need to close the gap to stop Adam Ashley-Cooper of Australia veering away.

ATTITUDE

Attitude is all about how a person acts, thinks or feels about something, so obviously a player's attitude towards rugby will determine how they play the game. Players should have a positive attitude, realizing that they will get out of rugby what they put in. Players should practise and play the game to the best of their ability, whether for themselves, their team, their club or any region or country they may represent.

KEY ELEMENTS
PROFESSIONALISM

Everything players do in rugby, whether they are students or paid professionals, they must try to do to the highest standards. That includes turning up on time and being prepared. The satisfaction gained from having a positive and professional attitude and always putting in your best effort can be most rewarding.

CONFIDENCE

Players gain confidence by knowing they have all the necessary skills, having learned and practised them thoroughly and to the best of their ability.

DECISION MAKING

Players should know that even if they are not the captain, they are still a decision maker and will be required to make decisions on the field, as necessary, for the benefit of their team.

A professional attitude includes respect for the opposition, for the officials and for yourself, as exemplified here by New Zealand All Black, Richie McCaw.

EFFORT

Players should give the maximum effort at all times and make no excuses. When things go wrong, they should learn from it so they are better next time.

ENJOYMENT

Players should enjoy their rugby because that is what it's all about: rugby is a game to be enjoyed. This element can be all too easily forgotten.

EQUIPMENT

Equipment should be looked after. That includes rugby boots (called "shoes" in North America), a mouthguard (also called a gumshield), uniform, sports bag and any padding or other clothing or accessories used for the game.

HEALTH

Players should also look after their bodies by keeping fit and maintaining a balanced and

Argentinean players enjoy a hard-fought victory against France.

The Samoan players perform their traditional war dance before a match.

A referee must be able to withstand a great many pressures and be fair to both sides.

healthy diet. Junk food and other unhealthy foods provide less energy and diminish an athlete's ability to play rugby.

REFEREES

Players should remember that referees are human. When refs make bad decisions players just have to put it behind them, get on with the game and make up for it by playing harder. Only the captain is allowed to query a referee's decision.

SPORTSMANSHIP

Players should respect the opposition and play fairly against them but do everything they can during the match to beat them. After the match, win or lose, they should behave sportingly with the opposition and develop friendships.

The touch judges assist the referees with decisions. They are the eyes and ears from the sideline.

Jérôme Thion of France tries to urge a decision out of the referee while trapped in a maul.

John Thiel of Canada and Nicky Little of Fiji chat after a game. Sportsmanship and friendship are an important part of rugby.

Even though heavily defeated, the Portugal players sportingly applaud the victors, the New Zealand All Blacks.

SPECIALIZED SKILLS

Along with the basic skills, there are two specialized skills in rugby that some players use a lot and some players use only occasionally. They are kicking and scoring a try.

KICKING

Done well, kicking the ball is a good way to make rapid progress up the field. Done badly, or too often, it gives away possession and allows the opposition an opportunity to attack. The three basic types of kick are the punt, the drop kick and the place kick. A punt is when the ball is dropped from the hands and kicked. A drop kick is when the ball is dropped from the hands and kicked as it hits the ground. In a place kick, the ball is placed on the ground and then kicked from that position.

THE PUNT

The punt is the kick used in general play. Kickers hold the ball in front of them and drop it a full leg's length away from the body to maximize the swing of the kicking leg. The non-kicking foot is planted firmly on the ground, and the kicking foot is drawn back behind the body then swung forward to make contact with the middle of the ball using the instep (the upper surface of the foot between the toes and the ankle). The head and shoulders are bent forward, and the eyes are fixed on the ball. The kicking foot strikes right through the ball.

Scotland fly half Dan Parks takes a kick at goal.

Juan Martin Hernandez of Argentina prepares to kick downfield.

Damien Traille of France is perfectly balanced for this punt. He has dropped the ball at the right height so his kicking foot can come forward and easily strike through it.

Frédéric Michalak of France punts the ball upfield as All Black Tony Woodcock tries to charge it down.

Jonny Wilkinson attempts a drop goal. TOP: As he drops the ball towards the ground, his kicking foot draws back. MIDDLE: His foot then comes forward to strike the ball as it hits the ground.

BOTTOM: To finish, his foot follows through, sending the ball in the direction of the goal.

THE DROP KICK

This is a specialized kick used to restart play and for kicks at goal (a field goal). The restarts are taken from the 22-metre line (22 metres is around 24 yards) for a dropout and the halfway line for a kickoff or restart.

In a drop kick, the ball is held vertically in both hands at about waist height. The kicker usually takes a single step forward then drops the ball, pointed end downward and tilted slightly backwards. The kicking foot is drawn backwards at the same time, and the foot swings forward to strike through the ball with the instep, a split second after the ball has bounced off the ground.

For longer kicks players lean into the ball. To loft the ball at kick restarts, kickers lean backwards and get their foot under the ball. This higher kick allows time for the forwards to make ground and try to win the ball.

THE PLACE KICK

The place kick is a specialized kick for taking a shot at goal — for a penalty or for a conversion attempt. Nowadays, most kickers place the ball on sand or a kicking tee and kick the ball with their instep. Every kicker has a personal style, but it usually involves placing the ball and then taking measured steps away from it. Then they usually look at the posts to visualize the ball going through them. The kicker should be calm and relaxed and ignore any distractions.

When ready, the kicker runs forward with measured steps, places the non-kicking foot firmly on the ground beside the ball and swings the kicking leg through an arc to strike the ball just above the ground. The player kicks right through the ball, the kicking foot swinging well past the point of contact.

Kicking a penalty.

TOP:
Jonny Wilkinson lines up a penalty kick attempt. The ball is upright on the kicking tee. He concentrates, visualizing what he expects to happen.

MIDDLE LEFT:
Dan Carter runs forward to kick the ball. His non-kicking foot will land near the ball, and his kicking foot will swing through to hit the ball.

MIDDLE RIGHT:
Just before impact, Jonny Wilkinson's shoulder comes forward over the ball.

BOTTOM LEFT:
Percy Montgomery's body is right over the ball, his kicking foot is kicking through it, and the ball is now travelling towards the goal.

BOTTOM RIGHT:
The final stage of a penalty kick.

OTHER TYPES OF KICKS

Kicking should always be done for a reason. Generally, a team will kick more often the closer they are to their own goal line (and less the closer they are to the opposition's goal line). These "other" kicks fall into three basic types, as shown in the diagram below:

- A — a defensive kick to get the ball out of a team's own 22-metre line (around 24 yards);
- B — a territorial kick from one's own half to get the ball into opposition territory;
- C — an attacking kick, which is often used when in the opposition's half to try to get behind, or wide of, the defensive line.

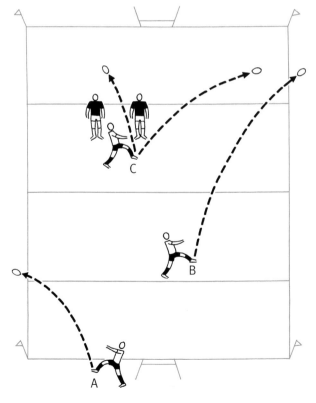

A: defensive kick
B: territorial kick
C: attacking kick

ACCURACY

The key to kicking is accuracy. Ideally, the ball will land in open space or fall into the arms of one of the attacking team's players who has run on to it. A good kick is a superb attacking weapon. A bad kick is also an excellent attacking weapon — for the opposition.

THE CHASE

There is a saying in rugby that the kick is only as good as the chase. The main chasers of a kick are usually the wingers, and they will often first have got a signal from the kicker. The winger must try to get to the ball as it lands back on the ground or on their side of the field within reach. Opposing players are allowed to compete for the ball in the air, but players cannot be tackled until they have caught the ball and landed back on the ground.

One tactic is to allow a player to catch the ball and then, immediately afterward, turn them or drive them to the ground with a well-timed tackle. However, it is not just the winger's job to chase kicks; all attacking players nearby should chase a kick and put pressure on the defending team.

THE CHIP KICK

This is a short punt in which the attacker chips the ball over the heads of the defenders. The attacker or a teammate then runs through the defensive line to chase the ball. This kick is sometimes called a chip-and-chase. The key to the chip kick is timing: when defenders are committed to a tackle or momentarily flat-footed, it is difficult for them to turn quickly and give chase.

KICKING TO TOUCH

When under sustained pressure inside their own 22-metre line, many teams will kick directly

All Black Dan Carter does a chip kick to get behind the opposition.

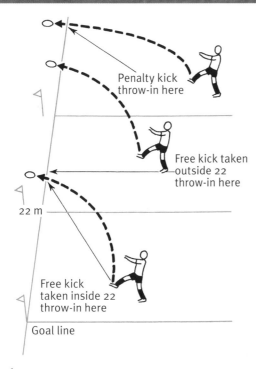

Penalty kick throw-in here

Free kick taken outside 22 throw-in here

22 m

Free kick taken inside 22 throw-in here

Goal line

to touch at the first opportunity. To do this effectively, kickers should try to send the ball directly out of play at a height that is above their opponent's reach. The distance gained is important, but in a desperate situation the priority is safety.

If the ball is kicked directly into touch from outside the 22, no ground is gained and the resulting line out is level from where the ball was kicked. So kickers should develop an awareness of where the touch-lines are and practise kicks that have the ball crossing the touch-line after one or more bounces in the field of play.

LEFT: Showing where a line out is taken from, when the ball is kicked out.

THE WIPERS KICK

Perhaps named after the side-to-side motion of a windshield wiper, this kick is an angled punt across the field in the direction of the open-side corner flag. It is used to change the direction of play and wrong-foot the opposition. It is particularly effective when play has become massed on one side of the field and the opposition has little defence on the other side. In this situation, a wipers kick will often dribble into touch undefended, making good ground and obtaining good field position for the attacking team.

THE CROSS KICK

This kick is similar to the wipers kick, except it is very flat and more of an attacking kick (while the wipers kick is more of a territorial kick). The cross kick is best used when the attacking side has more players out wide than the opposition has. The kick is made into space where unmarked players of the attacking side can run on to it.

THE SCREW OR SPIRAL KICK

The screw kick is a punt in which, rather than kicking right through the middle of the ball, the player kicks through the side of it, causing the ball to spin in flight. This reduces air resistance, allowing the ball to go farther through a flatter trajectory (the curved path of an object as it rises then starts to fall). The screw kick is effective when kicking to touch outside the 22-metre line because the spinning action can cause the ball to bobble into touch. It is also a good kick to use when kicking into a strong wind.

THE UP-AND-UNDER KICK

Also known as the Garryowen (after the Irish club that frequently used it), this kick is a punt in the opposition's half of the field. The ball is kicked

Both Mark Cueto of England and Victor Matfield of South Africa show good technique under this kick, but who will win it?

high into the air and just far enough upfield to allow players of the attacking team to contest possession when it comes down. The best placing of an up-and-under is just outside the opposition's 22, because one of the opposition could catch it and call for a mark inside the 22.

The up-and-under is a useful tactic in wet weather or if the opposition fullback, or one of the wings, is a poor catcher of high balls. In a tight defensive game, the up-and-under is often used to pressure the opposition and force them to make a mistake.

In a defensive situation, when the ball has been kicked to a fullback or wing and it is risky for them to run the ball, the fullback will often counterattack by doing an up-and-under. It gets the ball safely back into the opposition half and, if the kicker chases the kick, puts their own players in front, onside.

Perfect technique from Cédric Heymans of France, as he jumps and clutches the ball to his chest.

All Black Dan Carter does a grubber kick along the ground.

THE TAP KICK

The tap kick is an option when a team has been awarded a penalty kick. Rather than kick for goal or for the touch-line, the ball is held in both hands, released, tapped with the foot and immediately caught again by the kicker. The ball is now in play again, and the kicker can run forward or pass the ball.

THE GRUBBER KICK

The grubber kick is a punt in which the ball is kicked for a short distance along the ground. It is like a chip kick except that it stays low and is often bobbing around, and for this reason is difficult to defend against.

THE HACK KICK

The hack kick is used when the ball is loose on the ground and players have little chance of claiming it by hand, or when it is too risky to attempt a pickup when the ball is wet. Instead, an advantage might be gained by "hacking" the ball forward — soccer style — in order to pick it up in more space or with more time, or even hack it forward again, depending on the circumstances.

THE BOX KICK

This is a specialized kick usually used by the scrum half (or fly half) at a line out, scrum, maul or ruck. The scrum half kicks the ball high into the air in the direction of the opposing blind-side wing.

The scrum half's wing, usually alerted by a signal, sprints forward in an attempt to get to the ball first or put pressure on the opposition wing. The "box" is the open space in front of the blind-side wing and fullback and behind the forwards in a set-play situation.

Scrum halves must be skilled at kicking when their side has lost the momentum.

THE OVER-THE-SHOULDER KICK

A version of the box kick in which a scrum half, chasing backwards to collect a loose ball, has their back to the opposition and does a box kick over their shoulder before the opposition forwards can catch them in possession.

Lee Byrne of Wales dives to score.

KICKING IN WIND

When a ball is kicked into the air, it can be influenced by the wind. Before a match, a kicker should check how strongly the wind is blowing and in which direction.

One trick is to throw grass in the air and see which way it blows. Another is to wet a finger, hold it up in the air and feel which side gets cold (this will be the direction the wind is blowing from).

Kickers must use the wind to their team's advantage. When the wind is behind them, especially if it is strong, kickers should consider kicking more frequently (though still wisely).

SCORING A TRY

To score a try you hold the ball and fall over the opposition's goal line. Then you get up and shout with delight. Simple. But many tries have been lost because players have not used the proper technique to ground the ball when they are near or over the goal line.

GROUNDING THE BALL

The ball must be grounded with downward pressure on or over the opponent's line, using the

All Black Andrew Hore has run around to score close to the posts, to make the conversion easier for his kicker.

hands, arms or upper body. When ball carriers cross the goal line out wide, and there are no defenders close by, they should try to get closer to the posts to make the conversion attempt easier for the kicker. The ball can also be grounded against the pads of the posts.

LOW BODY POSITION

When trying to cross a defended goal line, players should get their body position as low as possible and drive for the line with the ball hugged safely to the chest. They should aim to ground the ball about a ball's length over the line in case the tackler knocks them back in the tackle. When players are about to be tackled from behind while

Bobby Skinstad of South Africa reaches out with one hand to score.

81

Juan Smith of South Africa keeps his body position low to just get over the line and score against Fiji.

Simon Webster of Scotland reaches out to score.

scoring, they too should keep their body position low to minimize the risk of the ball being jarred out in the tackle.

REACHING OUT

Normally, players must keep a firm grip on the ball when grounding it. But if tackled just short of the goal line, they are allowed to reach out for the line as long as they do so immediately. When scoring near the corner flag, the feet should be off the ground in the dive to avoid stepping on the touch-line. The ball has to be grounded before any part of the try-scorer's body touches the corner flag or the touch-line, or the ball will be "out". This skill should be practised by wingers and others who often score tries near the corner.

PUSH-OVER TRY

A push-over try comes from a scrum in which the attacking team pushes their opponents over the goal line. The number eight controls the ball with the feet, keeping it in the scrum until it is on or over the opponent's line, then they put a hand on the ball or fall on it to score the try. A try can also be scored from a ruck or maul in the same way.

PENALTY TRY

A penalty try is awarded by the referee when a defending team uses foul play to prevent what they consider would have been a certain try. The person who would have scored does not get the credit — the try is awarded to the team. The conversion attempt is then taken from in front of the posts.

England's Josh Lewsey scores an early vital try against France.

Frenchman Jérôme Thion's tackle is too late, as Frederico Aramburu of Argentina is over the line and will ground the ball.

THE SCRUM

All players must practise the individual skills appropriate to their playing positions. Skills that are practised with others are unit and team skills. Rugby is a very structured game that is divided into set play, phase play (second, third, fourth, and so on) and open play.

Set play (or a "set piece") is a way of restarting the game after a stoppage — after a team has scored, for example. Set play includes scrums, line outs, kick restarts, penalties and free kicks.

Phase play (more details are covered in chapter 11) is when the ball is contested in tackle situations, rucks and mauls. Phase means a stage. In the modern game, teams will deliberately set up a ruck or a maul to draw in defenders and regain possession of the ball before launching an attack.

Open play is uninterrupted play involving running, passing and kicking. It usually occurs in short bursts between set play and phase play. For example, from a scrum (set play) the attacking side breaks the opponent's line and, with running and passing (open play), advances forward to

A scrum is a pushing contest, here between the
New Zealand All Blacks and Fiji.

The French front row stays high, while the Argentinean scrum is packed low. Both will be trying to dictate how and when they come together for "the hit".

the opposition's 22-metre line, where one of the attackers is tackled and a ruck forms (phase play). The attacking team wins the ruck and now has the ball for a second phase (second-phase ball). The ball is passed out to the centres, a player is tackled and another ruck forms, which the same team also wins. Now they have the third-phase ball, and so on.

Continuous open play rarely lasts for long, but when it does, it can be hectic and the most thrilling part of rugby.

SCRUMS

The scrum is sometimes referred to as the engine room — the source of the power that drives the whole team. Success or failure in the scrum affects the whole team. The ability of the scrum to apply and absorb pressure influences the rucks and

mauls that follow it. For example, if a team has possession of the ball in the scrum and is going forward, it is easier for them to launch an attack. But if its forwards buckle under pressure, then the quality of possession will be poor, an attack will be less likely to succeed, and the forwards will probably be less energetic going into the next ruck or maul. A good scrum is a tightly bound, concentrated and disciplined unit, with each player having a role to play.

THE FRONT ROW

The whole scrum is akin to a blunt-nosed battering ram trying to force the opposition backwards. The front row is the face of that battering ram, not only having to push forward but also having to support their own players who are pushing from behind. The formation of the front row starts with the hooker. They raise their arms so that a prop

An aerial view showing the All Blacks and Canadian scrums about to engage.

The Fijian scrum. The front row is the point of impact, the second row does most of the pushing, the back row is first to leave the scrum and chase the ball.

on each side can tuck a shoulder underneath; the hooker then grips each prop by their jersey. In the same way, each prop puts their nearest arm around the back of the hooker so all three are tightly bound together.

At this point, the weight of the front row should be leaning slightly backwards to counter the weight of the second row and the back row who are joining the scrum behind them. The legs of the front row are splayed slightly outward, their knees slightly bent, their backs straight. They look straight into the eyes of the opposing front row. They should be mentally prepared for the impact when the referee sets the scrum. Their intention is to move forward, shoving the other team backwards.

THE SECOND ROW

If the scrum is the engine room, then the second row is the boiler room, providing the energy of the shove. Because they are bound in the middle of the scrum and are able to lean forward with their whole body length (unlike the props), they give the scrum most of its forward thrust. Before they join with the front row, the second rowers bind with each other in a similar fashion to the front row — linking arms around each other's backs. The second row forwards then place their innermost shoulder against the hooker's thighs and their other shoulder against the prop. They grip the prop with their free hand.

THE BACK ROW

The two flankers place their inside shoulders against the outside buttocks of the two props. They should push straight even though they are on the side of the scrum. Number eights put their shoulders up against the buttocks of the two second row forwards in front of them. Their arms go around their hips. They will be leaning full length like the second row. The scrum is now set and ready for engagement.

THE ENGAGEMENT

(See Law 20, pages 153–155, for the exact procedure.) The front row now crouches low but with the shoulders no lower than the hips. They will be about one arm's length away from the opposing forwards. The referee will tell the two sets of forwards to "touch". They will touch with their arms and then the ref will call "pause" and tell them to "engage". The two front rows will then impact against each other, their heads

This Scottish scrum is low and tightly bound.

The Italian and Portuguese scrums are engaged, waiting for the ball to be put in.

Eoin Reddan of Ireland is about to feed the ball into the scrum.

interlocking, with the two loosehead props from each team on the outside.

The players in the scrum should keep their backs straight and their legs slightly flexed, ready to push as soon as the scrum half puts the ball into the scrum. Scrum halves will often alert their own team by a coded call when the ball is about to be put in so they can begin to push before the other team. This coordination between the scrum half and the front row should be practised in training. Scrum halves should feed the ball into the scrum at a slight angle to make it easier for their own hooker to hook it back on their side.

Strength, technique and courage decide who wins the scrum's pushing contest. As in tackling, the whole body should be aligned to give maximum push, the back remaining straight. The position of the feet gives the front row forward both balance and thrust off the ground. In the front row, more than anywhere else, technique is important and is worth taking the time to get right, long before an opposed scrum is practised. If one team is obviously stronger in the scrums, then they will have an advantage and attempt to roll the other team backwards at every opportunity. This tires out the opposing forwards, gains territory and forces the opposing backs to retreat.

THE CHANNELS

The ball is put into the scrum by the scrum half. When the ball has been won by the hooker, the forwards have to channel the ball to the back of the scrum where the scrum half or number eight can pick it up. No one else is allowed to touch the ball until it has been cleared from the scrum.

There are three basic channels. The first (channel 1) is between the prop and the left flanker.

Scrum channels: the hooker (2) hooks the ball back to the forwards who must then channel it back through the scrum to the scrum half. Channel 3 is the safest option.

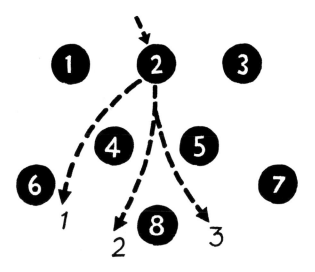

The British Lions flanker Martin Corry must remain bound until the ball has left the scrum.

This is not a very safe option because the opposing scrum half will be hovering there, waiting to pounce. The safest channel (3) is between the second row (the two locks) back to the number eight, who gets the ball on the right side; the player's bulk will protect it from the opposing scrum half. Not quite so safe is channel 2, where the the ball comes to the left of the number eight. This means that when it is picked up, the player will be facing the opposing number eight who is coming around the scrum.

THE DEFENSIVE SCRUM

The defensive scrum's role is almost the same as that of the attacking scrum. No matter who has the ball, both sets of forwards are trying to win the pushing contest. But as the ball moves back towards the channel, the loose forwards of the defending team should raise their heads (remaining bound, as the law demands) to see what the opposition is going to do with it.

As the tight forwards cannot always see when the ball has come free of the scrum, one of the loose forwards shouts to them when to break.

SCRUM PRACTICE

When practising scrummaging, coaches and players should spend time getting techniques exactly right, getting the feet exactly right and getting the back straight. If the basic techniques are perfected at an early age, players will scrummage correctly and safely all their lives. As soon as the basic techniques are mastered, weight and opposition can be added. Scrummaging should be practised both on a scrum machine and against real opponents. A scrum machine can be homemade, rather like a large sled, with padding for players to push against.

THE LINE OUT

The line out is a set way of getting the ball back into play after it has gone over the touch-line. Under the laws, the team to touch it last is the one that took it out of play (even if they did not mean to), and the other team gets to throw it back in (except when the ball is kicked out from a penalty).

KEY LINE-OUT SKILLS

The two sets of forwards line up about a metre (or a yard) apart, as shown in the diagram on page 94. The jumpers are usually the tallest players and the other players support them. The main jumpers normally stand at position numbers two, four and six, but this can be varied by the team throwing in.

THE THROW

These days it is the hooker who usually throws in the ball, although this can be varied. The ball can be thrown in any way as long as it goes in a straight line between the two rows of forwards. Most hookers take the ball back behind their

Argentina and South Africa contest a line out.

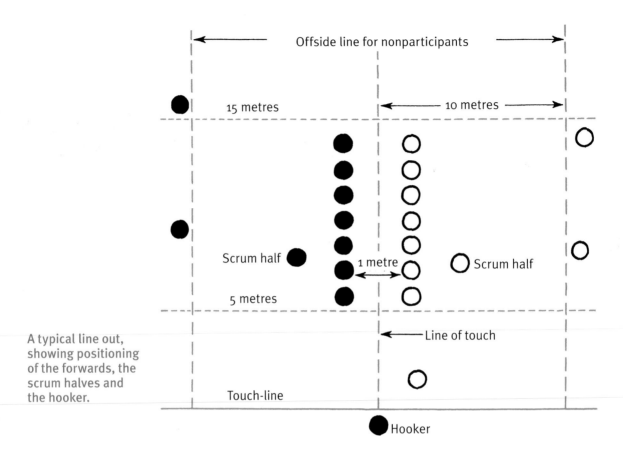

Offside line for nonparticipants

15 metres

10 metres

Scrum half

1 metre

Scrum half

5 metres

Line of touch

A typical line out, showing positioning of the forwards, the scrum halves and the hooker.

Touch-line

Hooker

head with both hands and then throw it forward with one or both hands. The ball has to go at least 5 metres (around 5$\frac{1}{2}$ yards).

THE CODE

Before the ball is thrown in, the attacking team decides which of their jumpers should catch it and what move they might attempt. One player — one of the forwards or the scrum half — will make the line-out calls, telling the other players the move by calling it out in code. Such a code might be a "magic number", decided before the game, that is used before the jumper's position in the line out. For example, if the magic number is three, then a call of "one, three, two" would mean the ball will be thrown towards the jumper standing at number

two because two comes after the magic number, three. The code should be repeated as necessary to make sure every player on the attacking team hears it. Teams should also have a backup code in case the opposing team is able to crack the first one. They can also use a silent signal, such as the scrum half putting one foot forward.

There is also a coded communication between the hooker and the jumper. Hookers can throw the ball flat or looped, quickly or with a delay. They will signal their intentions to the jumper with their body language — twitches, raised eyebrows or even the way they stand — and jumpers might respond in similar ways to indicate how they would like to receive the ball. These signals are previously agreed upon and practised in training. Hookers must throw the ball so that jumpers can

Sébastien Chabal of France waits at a line out. If he is the jumper, he will signal to his hooker.

A clean take at the line out by Hayden Mexted of the USA.

catch it at the top of their jump (unless a flat throw has been called).

THE JUMP

Jumpers must jump off both feet and be aggressive in trying to catch the ball. Their opponent will try to obstruct them, so they must be prepared for this. At the same time, they need to time their jump so they can take the ball cleanly.

There are three basic jumps. Jumpers can jump forward into the ball, jump straight into the air or backwards to take a looped throw from the hooker. If there is space, they can also take steps forward or backwards.

As soon as the jump is made, the props, or the props and other supporting players, hold the jumper up in the air to give the jumper more hang time and therefore more chance of catching the ball. As soon as the jumper has caught the ball, they must twist towards their own team to keep the ball away from the opposition. As the jumper lands, the supporting players must form a wedge on either side so the opposition are unable to get at the ball. The jumper should then hold on to the ball until instructed to release it by the scrum half.

VARIATIONS ON THE LINE OUT

THE ONE-HANDED TAP BACK

If jumpers can't get two hands on the ball, they should try to tap it back on to their side with their inside hand. (Players are not allowed to use only their outside hand to catch or tap the ball.)

An accurate tap back gets the ball back to the scrum half quicker and can set up an immediate attack. However, a wild one-handed tap back that does not go straight to the scrum half often turns the advantage over to the opposition, who come chasing through after it. One-handed taps back are particularly dangerous with a slippery ball in wet weather or near a team's own goal line.

THE SHORTENED LINE OUT

A normal line out consists of seven forwards from each side (the eighth forward is the thrower). The team throwing in the ball decides how many players make up the line out. A line out with less than seven is considered a "short line out". If the defending team uses more players than the attacking team, they will be penalized (if the referee or touch judges spot it).

A short line out must have at least two players from each side. Line outs might be shortened for several reasons: a team that has lost a lot of normal line outs may want to change things up, or a team may have a very good jumper who will do better with more space, or they want to do a special move that requires fewer players.

Assisted by his teammates, Isoa Domolailai of Fiji claims the ball with one hand.

All Black Chris Jack at full stretch, about to catch
the ball in two hands.

CHANGING POSITIONS

The main jumpers can be moved around in the line out to take up other positions. Depending on the defensive pattern a team uses, if the jumpers in the attacking team change position in the line out, so too will the jumpers marking them.

ADDING A PLAYER

The attacking team does not have to announce how many players are to stand in the line out — that is decided by the player who does the line-out calls. It is up to the defending team to count them and make sure they have the same number. Just before the ball is thrown in, a member of the attacking team can rejoin the line out to become a new jumper (and, therefore, may be unmarked).

THE THROW OVER THE TOP

The ball must be thrown straight down the gap formed between the two sets of forwards, but it can also be thrown straight over the top of them with a long and accurate throw. This would be a planned move (a move worked out and practised in advance), and a player from the attacking team, who was not in the line out, would come forward from a deep position to take the ball. But the throw must be straight.

THE QUICK THROW-IN

The team that has the throw-in can throw the ball in even before a line out is formed. Any player in that team can take the throw-in as long as they are the first in their team to touch the ball. The quick throw-in must be straight and taken from a position level with or behind where the ball went into touch.

Players are even allowed to throw the ball in and catch it themselves, but they must be sure to throw it over the 5-metre line (5 metres is around 5½ yards). The quick throw-in can be very effective because it can take the opposition by surprise.

LINE-OUT THROWING PRACTICE

Throwing the ball straight into the line out is probably the hardest skill to master in rugby. Like anything, it takes practice, and hookers should practise on their own time as well as at scheduled practices. The best way to practise throwing a line out is to first mark the side of one of the goalposts at the height at which the jumpers are at the top of their jump. Hookers should then measure back along the goal line and stand about 6 metres (6½ yards) back (which is the distance they would be throwing to the number two in the line out). They have 10 throws. How many times do they hit the goalpost? As they get more accurate, they can move back and measure so they are throwing to where the number four jumper would stand and then the number six jumper. Practise makes perfect.

BASIC MOVES FROM THE LINE OUT

THE PEEL

After the ball is thrown into the line out, the prop or another player peels off the front of the line out and runs back between the line out and the scrum half.

The catcher, instead of passing the ball to the scrum half, passes or taps it to the prop, who makes a charge along the end of the line into the opposition forwards or backs. The peel is also known as the Willie away, named after Wilson Whineray, the New Zealand forward who "invented" it.

THE BLIND-SIDE CHARGE

This move is similar to the peel, except this time the hooker, after throwing the ball into the line out, stays on the blind side (the 5-metre gap between the front of the line out and the touch-line). The ball is thrown back to the hooker (or another attacking player) by the successful jumper in the line out, who then charges through the blind-side gap, running down the touch-line.

THE WING COMES IN

In this move, after the line-out ball is won, the wing cuts back from the other wing (on the side where the line out takes place) to take the ball near to the end of the line out and charge at an angle towards the opposition backs.

DEFENDING A LINE OUT

Teams sometimes choose not to compete in line outs when lifting makes it easier for the team throwing in the ball to win it. In this case, the defending team should concentrate solely on stopping any forward drive by the opposition.

When a jumper in the defending team does compete, a one-handed tap back is

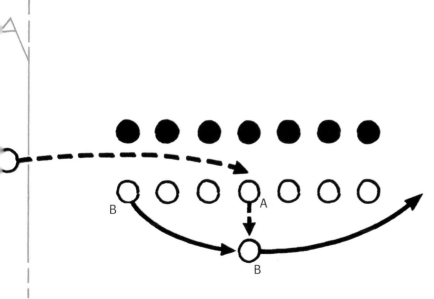

The peel: the ball is thrown down the middle of the line out. Player A catches it and passes it to player B, who has come from the front and now peels around the back with the ball.

As the line out is contested, the England players on the ground are coming around in support.

usually attempted. Players in the defending team should also try to burst through any gaps in the attacking team's line out to get to the ball, catch the scrum half in possession or just to put pressure on the opposing team. Defending jumpers, when leaping for the ball, should always do so aggressively; even if they don't get a hand on the ball, their actions will help to spoil the other team's possession. However, they are not allowed to barge the opposition or grasp them while they are in the air. Shoulder-to-shoulder contact is allowed.

The defending team's hooker should be marking the opposite hooker, who will be throwing the ball in. They should stay in that position immediately after the ball has been thrown in, ready to block any blind-side move by the opposing team.

Simon Easterby of Ireland and Lionel Nallet of
France compete for a line out.

KICK RESTARTS

The individual skills of kicking were covered in some detail in chapter 7, under specialized skills. This chapter is about how a team repositions itself for the kickoff and kick restarts in set play. It covers kickoffs, the 22-metre dropout and defending against penalties and tap penalties, and the conversion.

THE KICKOFF

At the kickoff, all members of the team that is kicking off should be behind the kicker. Usually, the forwards group together on one side to chase the ball as soon as it has been kicked to try to regain possession, but it is up to the kicking team to decide how they want to distribute their players. The defending team would normally try to follow the kicking team's distribution pattern and mark them accordingly.

The ball must be kicked with a drop kick over the opposition's 10-metre line (10 metres is around 11 yards), or the opposing team will get a scrum

At the kickoff, all of the players must be behind the kicker.

on the halfway line. Before they kick the ball, kickers should signal to their team the kind of kick to expect: whether the kick will send the ball just over the 10-metre line or deep towards the opposing 22-metre line, and whether it will go near the touch-line or away from the touch-line.

One or two of the fastest forwards should be the main chasers; their job is to get to the ball first and secure possession. To achieve this, they should time their run from well behind the kicker so they can be almost at full speed when they come level with the kicker. Sometimes one of the wings is the main chaser.

THE 22-METRE DROPOUT

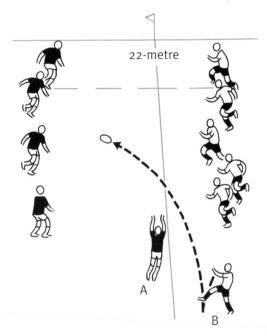

The 22-metre dropout.

This drop kick is similar to the restart from the halfway line, except it has to be taken anywhere behind the 22-metre line, as shown in the diagram opposite. At least one member of the opposing team (player A) will try to obstruct the kicker (player B) or charge down the ball, but they are not allowed to cross the 22-metre line.

Kickers can drop kick the ball high into the air for their own forwards to jump to and regain possession. These days though, teams usually go for a long kick into the opposition half, and the defending wingers should be prepared for this. This option has been chosen by the kicker in the diagram.

Sometimes teams do tricky little dropouts to try to win back possession of the ball — such as the kicker kicking it only just over the line, along the ground, to a teammate standing close by — but these moves are riskier than the long kick.

DEFENDING
AGAINST TAP PENALTIES

Once a referee has awarded a penalty, a frequent mistake made by the defending team is to drop their heads in disappointment, lose their concentration or even turn their backs to the opposition. Even though the referee has blown the whistle, the game has stopped only long enough for the penalty to be taken, and the attacking team might take a tap kick immediately.

As soon as a penalty has been awarded, defending players still on their feet should retire the regulation 10 metres (11 yards) to be prepared for the quick tap. Those who are on the ground should get to their feet as quickly as possible and do the same. Whatever happens, they should be alert to the possibilities. Always expect the unexpected.

With intense concentration, Shotaro Onishi of Japan prepares to kick a penalty.

remain in a line so that no gaps appear. If the tap penalty is taken 10 metres (11 yards) from the defender's goal line, the defending team must definitely charge forward, otherwise momentum will take the attackers over the line.

AGAINST A PENALTY KICK AT GOAL

The defenders must stand at least 10 metres (11 yards) back from a penalty kick at goal and are not allowed to charge. However, they must remain alert: if the kicker misses the game continues. Some of the defending team's best kickers should be positioned near the posts, in case the ball falls short or bounces back into play off the post or crossbar and they have to kick it to touch. If an unsuccessful penalty kick lands in the goal area, a defending player will usually force the ball down for a 22-metre (24-yard) dropout. Sometimes catchers might choose to run the ball back into the field of play before kicking to touch (from inside their own 22), or they might link up with other members of their team to create an attacking move. However, the touch down for a dropout is usually the safer option. In rugby union, a touch down is when a defender touches the ball on the ground in their own in-goal area. This can be done with any part of the body.

AGAINST THE FORWARD CHARGE FROM A TAP PENALTY

A team will often use a tap penalty to start a forward charge in order to gain ground before the ball is released for a second-phase attack. To counter this, the defending forwards should face their opposites, lined up about one metre (around a yard) apart. As soon as the attacking team has taken the tap penalty, the defending players can rush forward to make the tackle. But they must make sure they

AGAINST THE CONVERSION

Defending against a conversion is the same as defending against a penalty kick at goal, except that the defending team must stand behind the goal line. Players are allowed to charge, but only once the kicker starts to run. If the kicker starts to run, then stops, opposing players can still charge, even if the ball has fallen off the kicking tee.

11. PHASE PLAY

PHASE PLAY

In modern rugby, teams try to keep possession of the ball for long periods of time. If a team puts the ball into the scrum and wins that scrum, they have retained possession of the ball and are in the first phase of play.

If the ball is passed out to the centre, the centre is tackled and the attacking team retains possession of the ball after the ensuing ruck or maul, then the attacking team have created what is called second-phase ball. If the attacking team continue to hold on to the ball, then each successive ruck or maul for which they maintain possession is known as the third, fourth and fifth phase, and so on.

Set play is very structured, phase play is less so and in between is the more exciting play known as open play. At the higher levels of modern rugby, most of a match comprises phase play. One team tries to keep possession of the ball, and the other team tries to force them to make a mistake so they can get their hands on it. When they succeed, it is called a turnover. The three contact points of phase rugby are the tackled ball situation, the maul and the ruck.

This tackle is going to ground. The ball carrier can place the ball if he does so immediately, but neither he nor the tackler can play the ball until they get to their feet.

The Scotland fullback has gone to ground but is allowed to immediately place the ball.

TACKLED BALL

The ball carrier is about to be tackled. There is not enough space to slip the tackle, no teammate in support to pass to and a kick will lose the team's possession of the ball, so the carrier elects to take the tackle. The carrier has to try to set up the next phase so the team retains possession of the ball.

The first decision to be made is whether to attempt to stay upright and form a maul or go to the ground and form a ruck. The ball carrier should never go to ground if there is no support close by, as opposing players on their feet will have the right to play the ball and the ball carrier won't. (However, if the tackle is good and takes the carrier to ground anyway, this decision is already made.)

Ball carriers who remain on their feet and are strong may decide to form a maul. If they are outnumbered by opponents, then they should try to stay on their feet until their teammates arrive. This is because if the ball carrier goes to ground, the ball must be placed or released immediately and, consequently, will likely be surrendered to the opposition.

If ball carriers do stay on their feet, they should try to turn the ball towards their team-mates and away from the opposition. If players bind on to them, the tackled ball situation becomes a maul.

Whatever decision ball carriers make, they must do their best to present the ball back to their own team and use their body to shield the ball from the opposition.

Players are on the ground so it is likely a ruck will form.

As South Africa's Schalk Burger goes to ground, players of both sides are close, so it is likely they will form a ruck over him.

Ireland's Frankie Sheahan is on the ground. A ruck has not yet formed over him, so players on their feet are allowed to try to pick up the ball and Sheehan must release it.

THE BREAKDOWN

The situation immediately following a tackle is called the breakdown. It is the least understood and most argued part of rugby — and it is where the most penalties are conceded. Even so, the laws are quite straightforward.

TACKLED PLAYER BROUGHT TO GROUND

When tackled players are brought to the ground and are held in the tackle, they must place or release the ball immediately. (If they are not held in the tackle, they can get up and start running again.) As soon as tackled players release the ball, the tackler must release them

because they no longer have the ball. Tackled players can then get to their feet and pick up the ball again.

TACKLER MUST ROLL AWAY

Once the tackler has made the tackle and released the tackled player, the tackler must roll out of the way so as not to illegally prevent the other team from getting the ball.

TACKLER'S RIGHT TO COMPETE

Once they have made the tackle, the tacklers have the right to compete for the ball as long as they are on their feet. They must immediately get to their feet — both feet, not one foot and one knee

If the South African number five joins with the two players on their feet, this will become a maul. A maul must consist of at least three players on their feet (at least one player from each team). At present it is not a maul because one of the three is on the ground.

— before attempting to pick up the ball. This is complicated by the fact that, as tacklers try to pick up the ball, opposition players will be coming in, trying to drive them off their feet. Referees need very good judgement to decide if tacklers are actually on their feet or not.

JOINING THE BREAKDOWN

New players arriving at the breakdown, whether it be a ruck or a maul, must enter from the rear, and they must bind with the players who are already a part of it. Players who are not in the ruck or maul should be behind the feet of the players at the back of it, or they will be offside.

THE MAUL

If tackled players are still on their feet when the first of their teammates arrive at the breakdown, these players must form a wedge around them and support them on each side, shielding the ball from the opposition. Other teammates do the same, widening the wedge to provide a screen that will prevent the opposition from getting anywhere near the ball.

When a tackle is made in the back line and the forwards are slow to arrive, the backs must engage in the maul to form a wedge that will keep the opposition away from the ball. Backs should

If all players remain on their feet in this tackle situation, it is a maul.

Australia rolls the maul forward trying to penetrate the Canadian defence.

practise this in training. Sometimes the first player to arrive will take the ball off the tackled player and a maul might form around that player.

STRIPPING THE BALL

Often a maul is part-formed with an opposition player still wrestling for the ball. In this case, the opposition player should be driven back or squeezed away from the ball. When trying to wrestle the ball from another player, the force of the whole body should be used, shoulder first, to wrench the ball away.

THE DRIVING MAUL

The purpose of the maul is to secure possession, but if the maul is going forward, the attacking side — usually instructed by their scrum half — might decide to continue driving forward to gain ground. The ball should be carried by a player in the second row or at the back of the maul to protect it from the opposition. In this kind of maul, the leading forwards may be fairly upright, but those behind should adopt a low body position to push the maul forward.

The drive should be continued for as long as the maul is moving forward. Once the maul becomes stationary a change of tactics must be employed: either the ball is released to the backs or it is moved to other players in a position to continue progress with a rolling maul (see page 114). Failure to make use of the ball once the maul has stopped going forward may result in the referee stopping play and handing possession to the other side under the "use it or lose it" rule.

THE ROLLING MAUL

The rolling maul is similar to the driving maul, except that when the maul becomes stationary the attacking team smuggles the ball to the side of the maul where the defence seems weakest (the ball must always travel backwards, of course). The player with the ball then rolls out to the side, tightly supported by teammates. As soon as the new unit makes ground, the other forwards peel off the original maul and support the new movement.

As the defending team regroups and "plugs the gap", the ball is again smuggled to another part of the maul to change the point of attack. A rolling maul can continue indefinitely in this way, but the attacking team should not continue it for too long since they risk losing the ball.

The rolling maul should be coordinated by the scrum half, who has the best view of what is going on. The scrum half should be talking to the forwards continuously, telling them where the defence is weakest and instructing other players where to add their support. The best line of attack in a rolling maul is often the side opposite to where the ball originally came from.

A rolling maul is often a good tactic for scoring a try from a line out near the opponent's line.

The South African pack is in perfect formation for this driving maul.

TRUCK AND TRAILER

The attacking side must maintain contact with the opposition in a rolling maul. If contact is broken, the attacking players in front of the ball are deemed to be obstructing the opposition players who are trying to get to the ball, which is being held in the second rank. The two groups from the attacking team must also be in contact with each other, otherwise the referee will award a penalty against them for creating a "truck and trailer". This describes a maul that, instead of being one maul is in two parts, with the "truck" at front protecting the ball-carrying "trailer" behind.

THE RUCK

A ruck is a loose scrum formed in open play. The original meaning of the word ruck is "a heap", and so a ruck came to mean a heap of bodies all trying to get the ball off the ground. The modern ruck was developed in the 1940s, when Vic Cavanagh, who was the coach of the Otago provincial team in New Zealand at that time, organized his forwards into a loose scrum that drove over the ball on the ground. From there the technique spread all over the world as a way of gaining possession of the ball that was faster

The ball carrier (number three) has been tackled to the ground. Now players from both sides form a ruck over him to try to push each other off the ball.

A ruck between Argentina and Namibia. The players must stay on their feet or risk being penalized.

than a maul. It gives the attackers an advantage as the defenders have less time to regroup.

THE START OF THE RUCK

A ruck is formed when at least two opposing players are in contact with each other over a loose ball on the ground. As soon as a ruck is formed it is illegal to use the hands until the ball comes out of the ruck. Either the feet must be used to hook the ball back or the players can drive forward and step over the ball so that it comes out on their side.

CREATING A RUCK

In the modern game, players often deliberately create a ruck by falling to the ground in, or just prior to, a tackle. They lie with their body shielding the ball from the opposition, making it easier for their own team to regain possession. Players who fall to the ground are allowed to use their hands to place the ball on the ground or push it towards their own team, as long as they do it immediately and do not hang on to it. The ruck is formed as players from both sides come together over the loose ball.

Ideally, the first wave of support players from the attacking team drop their shoulders and bind together, as in a scrum, a pace or two before they hit the ruck. With short pumping steps, they attempt to step over the player and the ball and drive the opposition players back. Other forwards then join the ruck, binding on to their teammates. The secrets to success are the low body position (shoulders level with or just a little higher than the hips) and being tightly bound together (the old saying is that they should be so close that you could throw a blanket over them).

A ruck is not really a pushing contest like a scrum. The team whose forwards form up and start driving first will usually win the ruck. Sometimes the ball becomes stuck in the ruck behind bodies that are in the way and an attacking team needs to dig the ball out with their feet. This has to be done carefully so as not to injure any players lying on the ground, as referees have different interpretations of this technique and may award a penalty for dangerous play.

If opposing forwards are hanging on to the side of the ruck, the attacking players in the ruck can bind on to them and pull them into the ruck, so preventing them from spoiling the ball as soon as it is freed. If the first wave of forwards has control of the ruck, then players arriving late should not enter the ruck but position themselves just behind it, waiting to see what develops. As in a maul, the ruck should be controlled by the scrum half, who has the best view of it.

CLEARING A RUCK

Because a ruck ball is a fast, attacking ball, scrum halves must clear the ball fast or the advantage will be lost. Sometimes they will spread the ball quickly out to the backs (the players at the back of the ruck), who can time their runs better because they can see the ball coming. Sometimes scrum halves will just pop the ball up to the forwards standing nearby, who will charge forward and set up the next ruck or maul. If the opposition forwards are out of position, a series of rucks can be continued down the field.

Because of the nature of the ruck, the scrum half may not always be available to pass the ball (they might still be getting up from the last ruck), so any player in the attacking team must be prepared to act as scrum half when the ball pops out of the ruck.

PICK-AND-GO

Pick-and-go is a fast and specialized form of rucking in which an attacking player, obstructed by a defender, goes to the ground and forms a ruck. Several teammates then drive any opposition players off the ball, leaving the ball on the ground behind them (this is called "blowing over"). Another forward then picks up the ball and goes forward to create the next ruck in the same way. The process is then repeated, often several more times, as the forwards work their way up the field.

12. DEFENCE

DEFENCE

Defence is based on systems, of which there are three basic types in modern rugby: player-on-player, drift defence and rush defence. Variations of these can be used in specific situations, such as defending a move off the back of the scrum near a team's own goal line. It is crucial that every player on the team is aware of the pattern used, and sticks to it in the pressure of a match situation.

PLAYER-ON-PLAYER DEFENCE

In player-on-player defence, the players of a defending team tackle the player directly opposite them, as shown in diagram 1 on page 121. But if the fullback enters the line, then the inside player nearest them takes them. There is also a variation of player-on-player defence in which the open-side flanker takes the fly half, especially when their own fly half is not a good tackler. After that each player takes their own opponent.

An aerial view of two back lines opposing each other.

DRIFT DEFENCE

In drift defence (diagram 2, opposite), the open-side flanker (white 7 in the diagram opposite) comes off the scrum or the back of the line out to challenge the opposing fly half (black 10). The defending team's fly half (white 10) then takes the opposition's inside centre (black 12) and so on. Therefore, the defending team's players are not taking the player opposite them but the next one out and they have to "drift" across the field to make the tackle.

This drifting angle pushes the attacking team sideways across the field towards the touch-line, giving them less space to work in. It also allows for an extra player in the defensive team to take the fullback if they enter the line. This extra player would normally be the outside centre, but if the fullback comes into the line in another position, one of the other players would have to tackle them. Also, the angle of the drift follows the ball, so if the ball carrier passes, then the tackler is running in the right direction to make the tackle.

This type of defence is also known as player-out defence or one-out defence, because the tackler is tackling the player outside them.

A variation of this is the outside-in defence, in which the defensive pattern starts marking players from the wing inward, towards the scrum. In this variation, tacklers are lining up on the outside shoulder of their opponent, coming at them on an angle.

• DEFENCE IS A TEAM RESPONSIBILITY
• TACKLING IS AN INDIVIDUAL RESPONSIBILITY

The five major components of a defensive plan are marking, tackling, communication, concentration and discipline:

1. Marking — In a defensive line, every player in the team is responsible for marking a member of the opposing team (usually the one who is standing opposite them). That means covering that player and staying with them, almost like a mirror image, then quickly closing them down when they are about to receive the ball.

2. Tackling — When an opposition player gets the ball, the defender marking that player must make an effective tackle.

3. Communication — Situations can change rapidly in rugby. An attacking side can change its angles, run decoys and use all sorts of deceptive ploys to try and trick the opposition. The defence counters this by shouting to each other to let players know who is marking whom.

4. Concentration — Defence is less exciting than attack. It takes concentration and hard work. Usually it only lasts for a short period before the defenders get the ball and become the attackers again. It is very satisfying to halt an opposition attack and stop them from scoring.

5. Discipline — Defence is discipline. Players talk about "muscling up" in defence, but muscling up is as much a mental application as it is a physical one.

1. Player-on-player defence

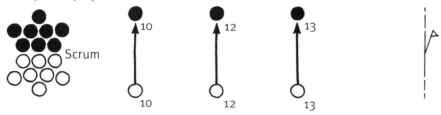

2. Drift defence or player-out/one out

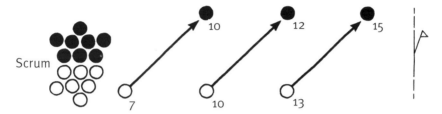

3. Blind-side defence

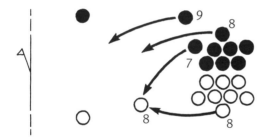

Blind-side defence: the number eight (white) attacks down the blind side. The defending (black) blind-side flanker (7), number eight (8) and scrum half (9) must come across and defend.

Fijian players are positioned low, ready to defend their goal line.

RUSH DEFENCE

Rush defence is a form of outside-in defence in which the defenders rush up rapidly on the attackers. Because they are aiming towards the outside shoulder and the ball is coming from the inside, the attackers are looking the wrong way, which puts them under more pressure.

BLIND-SIDE DEFENCE

The key to stopping an attack that comes down the narrower channel of the blind side of the field is an early tackle. This is the responsibility first of the blind-side flanker (black 7, in diagram 3 on the previous page), supported by the scrum half (black 9) and the number eight. Scrum halves should be communicating with the back row as soon as they see the opposition making a blind-side attack.

Defending wingers on the blind side usually hang back, marking the opposing winger, but if the other defenders are slow, or if they read the move early, they can rush in and make the tackle, but they have to make sure the tackle will be successful before they start their run, or they will leave a huge gap behind them.

DEFENSIVE SYSTEMS

A team's defensive systems are set before a match. In broken play, however, depending on the circumstances and how their opponents are lined up in attack, players will make a change and call different systems as necessary. The backs are more used to this, and at such times they should direct the forwards where to stand or which opponent to take.

PRACTISING DEFENCE

At training, teams often practise attacks going forward. They should also practise defence going backwards. Players should know where they are supposed to be and what they are supposed to do in all defensive situations. They should be challenged and pressured just as they would be in a real match.

BELOW: All Blacks Jerry Collins and Luke McAlister
ready themselves in defence.

OPPOSITE: Fijian Sevens player Stefano Cakau
fends off the Canadian defender on his way to
score.

ATTACK

The most exciting part of rugby is the attack, and the ultimate aim of attacking is to score tries. Attacking plans should be based on the strengths of the personnel in the team, such as a strong centre or a fast winger. The attacking team should have several moves they can use in a match, but their attacks should also be unpredictable and difficult for the opposition to read.

Attacks should be launched towards open space; if that space becomes defended, another attack should be launched into wherever the space now is. Generally, the most space is to be found at the edges of the field.

PARTS OF AN ATTACK

There are four basic parts to an attacking move: the roles played by the playmaker, the penetrator, the supporters and the finisher.

The playmaker is the player who creates the time or space to launch the attack.

New Zealand All Black Dan Carter has support as he runs in a try.

Vincent Clerc of France is all concentration as he catches the ball to score.

The penetrator is the player who breaks through, or penetrates, the opposition's defensive line. The supporters are all the other players in the attacking team who assist in the attack. The supporters often do the build-up work, wearing away the opposition defence and committing them to tackles, or rucks and mauls. Then the playmaker (with a dummy or delayed pass, or some other piece of deception) sets up a situation in which the penetrator is able to take advantage of a gap and run through it. The finisher is the one who scores, but also sometimes the one who sets up the final part of the try.

These role descriptions are general guidelines explaining how the roles could work in a successful attack. In a real situation, such as a solo run, the try scorer might be the playmaker, penetrator and finisher all in one. Any player can take on any of these roles. A number eight might penetrate the line with a surging run, a prop might be the playmaker and kick the ball through for the winger to run on to and, of course, anybody can score a try.

PENETRATING THE DEFENCE

Rugby has been described as chess with muscles. Both teams manoeuvre their pieces (players) around the field in an attempt to force the opposition to move their pieces in such a way that they leave holes in their defensive line.

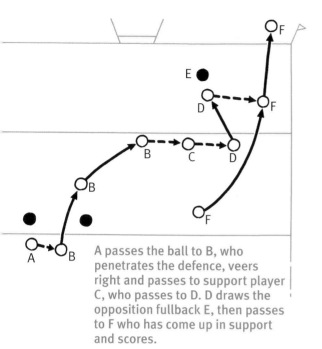

A passes the ball to B, who penetrates the defence, veers right and passes to support player C, who passes to D. D draws the opposition fullback E, then passes to F who has come up in support and scores.

The first objective is to get behind the opposition's defensive line. Players that do this are penetrators, but unless they are very fast and deceptive runners they are usually not the finisher. They still have to beat the second line of defence, the fullback and any covering players, which is why penetrators need support players to come through and back them up.

Usually, midfield backs are used as the playmakers or penetrators and feed the ball to the fast wingers, or wings, outside them, who are the finishers. The back three (the wings and the fullback) are usually used as finishers. When fullbacks come into the line, they should be running fast to maximize their chances of breaking through.

PENETRATORS NEED PACE

The key to attacking rugby is pace. The great Welsh coach Carwyn James used to say that you can defend against everything except pace.

Bryan Habana on his way to score a try for South Africa against Samoa.

Drew Mitchell of Australia tries to weave his way through the Fijian defence.

Andrea Masi of Italy gets out of one tackle but another looms, and he might need support to continue the attack.

All Black Rodney So'oialo has won the line out, but because he is falling, this is likely to be poor quality possession.

The most speed and the most space are usually on the wing. That is why wingers usually lead the try-scoring lists.

FINISHING

Finishing off an attack and scoring is a great skill. It takes killer instinct and concentration to take the opportunity and follow it through to a score. Good finishing is the mark of a very good team.

QUALITY BALL

When possession is won, the ball might come back to the attacking team advantageously, or it might come back scrappily. An advantageous ball is called quality ball (also known as front-foot ball). A bad ball is called bad or poor quality ball —

A secure take by Ali Williams will give the All Blacks good quality possession to work with.

Sean Lamont of Scotland breaks through against Portugal.

or names far worse! Quality ball is when the ball is freed to the scrum half (or someone in that position) quickly and cleanly, allowing the attacking team to immediately launch the next attack.

Bad ball is when it comes back slowly or untidily and slows the attack or even places the attacking side under pressure. Planned moves that have been worked out in advance should be canceled when bad ball means the move will have little chance of success. One solution for bad ball is to start again — create another ruck or maul, set up the next phase of possession and, hopefully, deliver better quality ball. When the quality of the ball is so bad that it puts the attacking team under extreme pressure, then the only option is to kick.

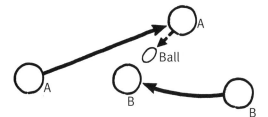

A scissors pass: Player A runs in front of teammate B and then passes back.

BREAKING THE LINE

The miss-out or cut-out pass bypasses a player in the attacking line, spreading the ball wide more quickly.

In the scissors or cut-back pass, ball carriers cut across in front of one of their own players and then twist to pass it back to their teammate (the lines of

All Black Brendan Leonard makes an intercept that will lead to a counterattack against Australia.

the two players cross each other like the blades of an open pair of scissors). The player who ends up with the ball can effectively change the angle of attack.

An overlap is created when players of the attacking team outnumber the opposing defence, allowing the "extra" player to get through (or to get past) unopposed.

A loop is a way of creating an extra player. The ball carrier passes the ball then runs around behind the receiver to take another pass.

In the pickup from the scrum, the number eight picks up the ball from the scrum and breaks towards the blind or open side, supported by the scrum half and the nearest flanker.

A blind-side attack is a very useful way of gaining a territorial advantage, especially when there is a

wide blind side and the ball is put into the opposite side of the scrum. If the attackers can run or pass the ball wide of the blind-side flanker, they have only the wing to beat in the first line of defence.

Decoy runs are a way to deceive the opposition at the point of attack. For example, when planning a blind-side move, the attacking fullback can make an open-side run as though expecting the ball to be going that way.

The fullback coming into the line is an excellent way of creating an extra player, changing the angle of the attack or increasing the pace of the attack.

The wing coming into the line has the same effect as the fullback coming into the line: the wing comes off the wing position into a new position in the line to create an extra player.

British Lions halfback Dwayne Peel launches a sudden attack.

Changing the angle of attack is one of the most effective ways of disrupting a defence. A typical example is the outside centre running out of space, changing direction towards the corner, then passing to the wing, who will cut in behind (a scissors move) and head for the goalposts.

The scrum-half dash is often a good option when channels of attack open up close to a scrum, ruck or maul. Scrum halves with good leg speed can often start an attack through these narrow gaps. The general rule is that scrum halves should run at least once a half to keep the opposition defence honest.

Communication is as important on attack as it is on defence. Players call moves, such as to come in for a pass, run forward during kicks and so on.

When in support, they call out to ball carriers to let them know they are there.

COUNTERATTACK

A counterattack is a quick response to an opposition attack after the attacking team has lost possession. Sometimes it is safer to kick the ball to touch but, just as often, if the defending team has players of genuine pace and the other team is stretched in defence, an immediate attack can be launched. If this is done at speed, a try can be scored or a territorial advantage gained. Rapid counterattacks can be very effective because the team that was on the attack will be slow reorganizing their defence. It is also thrilling to watch.

THE BEST OPTION

One of the hardest skills to teach in rugby is picking an option — that is, choosing between several alternatives. The team that takes the best options will invariably win the match. Of course, the best option to take depends on the circumstances. In a close match, neither team can afford to take risks.

If one team is ahead, they should generally take fewer risks to protect their lead. However, the team that is behind might have to take more risks in order to catch up. The player picking the option simply has to calculate the risks against the rewards and make the best decision for the team.

PICKING AN OPTION

In many situations, however, there is often only one obvious option, as outlined below.

DEFENDING ON OWN LINE — SITUATION ONE
Situation: A team is under great pressure on its own line and gets the ball.
Best option: Kick it to touch.

Under pressure inside his own 22, England's scrum half Andy Gomarsall kicks for the safety of the touch-line.

ATTACKING TWO ON ONE — SITUATION ONE

Situation: The ball carrier is facing the opposition fullback. Outside, the wing is unmarked.
Best option: The ball carrier draws the fullback and passes to the wing.

However, if the situation is different, the best option to take will also be different.

DEFENDING ON OWN LINE — SITUATION TWO

Situation: A team is under great pressure on their own line and get the ball. Time is up on the clock, and they are behind by three points.
Best option: Run the ball and try to keep it alive. The only chance of winning the game is to score at the other end of the field.

ATTACKING TWO ON ONE — SITUATION TWO

Situation: The ball carrier is facing the opposition fullback. Outside, the wing is also marked, but the fullback is coming up fast in support.
Possible option: Kick behind the opposing wing so the attacking fullback can run on to the ball.

OPTIONS AFTER SCORING

Most teams get too relaxed immediately after scoring and often give away a try. The opposition will take the kickoff and, in most instances, the team that has just scored should simply catch the ball and try to boot it into touch in the opposition's territory. This lessens the fired-up opposition team's ability to immediately bounce back.

TACTICAL OPTIONS

The tactics for a match are always based on the strengths of your own team and the weaknesses of the opposition. During the course of a game, tactics consist of doing more of what is working

This Argentinean forward catches the ball from a kickoff — an essential skill in order to regain possession after a score.

The England team huddle to discuss what they are going to do before a match.

(for example, blind-side attacks) and less of what is not working (for example, kicking the ball to the opposition fullback who is a fast runner). It is also about staying open to the possibilities, seeing the opportunities and taking them.

TACTICAL STRATEGIES

The attacking team is trying to cut loose, and the defence is seeking to stifle the opposition's attacks. With the tactics used, each team is trying to break the spirit of their opposition and convince the players that they cannot win.

SPIRIT

A team must have a strong and unified spirit: if one person makes a mistake, the team should feel they have all made a mistake; when one person scores, the whole team should consider they have scored. There should be no complaining about teammates and no excuses during a game. However, at the next training session players should be able to state the facts honestly — for example, X dropped a vital kick and may need more practice at that.

LEADERSHIP

A team will not be successful if they go on to the field and only do what the coach says. A team should certainly follow the coach's plan during a match, but, if that plan is clearly not working, they should not wait until the halftime talk to change it. People need to step forward as leaders. The coach will normally choose a captain and a pack leader (the leader of the forward pack), but there should also be other leaders on the team. Leaders are players who can see for themselves, think for themselves, come up with a solution and act on it without having to ask anybody's permission (though if there is time, they would tell their teammates first). Then, right or wrong, they take responsibility for the result. If they're wrong, they simply learn from the mistake and do it better next time, but they should not be frightened of making difficult decisions.

COACHING

A coach is a leader, teacher and guide and sets the standard. The coach should continually challenge the players and seek to improve them, both as players and as people. This will result in better performance of the team as a whole.

TEAM SELECTION

The first rule of team selection is "select either the player for the plan or the plan for the player". When putting a team together, decide what ingredients you require and set down the requirements for each position. Write these down and keep going back to them as you search for and select your players. Exhaust every avenue until you find the players that most closely match your requirements.

GOALS

Once the players are identified and notified, they must be part of a long-term goal. The management

A coach must bring the best out of the players. Here Brian Ashton talks with England team members.

The New Zealand All Blacks and France run out on to the field together.

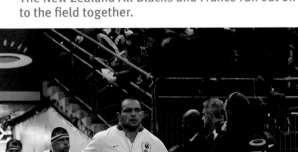

team, captain, vice-captains, players' committee, senior players and all members of the squad should all know and agree with the team's long-term goal. There must be no hidden agendas.

The long-term goal is achieved by setting and meeting short-term goals. Short-term goals must be realistic. Even smaller goals can then be set, which might be performance-related rather than scoreboard-related. Keep things basic and keep things simple. Improved performance leads to improved results. The most effective plan evolves slowly so that there is a continuous but gradual improvement throughout the team.

YOU AS COACH

- Be honest, both to yourself and your players. Never lie to them and if you need to criticize them, tell it straight.
- You are the coach, the guide and the manager, but your most important role is not as a talker but as a listener, because you are also the problem solver.
- Don't try to do it all yourself. Share the problem and use the abilities of the team to help solve it.
- Don't be too proud. If you don't know how to solve a problem a player is experiencing, find someone who can.

THE PLAYERS

- Raise your players' self-esteem and always strive to maintain it.
- Stimulate the players and encourage them to think about and discover their own solutions to problems. Encourage an open mind.
- Ensure each player knows their role. Test them on it. Don't let them get confused.
- Be realistic. It is unreasonable to expect excellence right away. Don't undermine your players' confidence by expecting them to be of a high standard too soon.
- Get them to seek improved performance ahead of seeking results on the scoreboard.

TRAINING

- Practices should be planned. Write down the tasks on cards and keep the cards for later reference. Be organized and stick tightly to times and schedules.
- Structure the practice so it involves the whole squad. Work on communication and teamwork. Aim for mistake-free activity. Make it enjoyable.
- Tell the players what you want to achieve at the beginning of each training session.
- Share the "voice load" at practice. Get the players to take responsibility for some of it.
- Encourage players to communicate constructively about the tasks at hand but be firm about idle or destructive chatter.
- Do the accuracy drills early in training, as the fatigue players experience later in the session will reduce their thinking and skill levels.

TEAM PATTERN

The first thing the coach and the team have to do is decide on the pattern of rugby they wish to play. They have to answer five basic questions:

- How are we going to win possession of the ball?
- How are we going to retain possession of the ball?
- How are we going to use the ball?
- What defensive patterns will the opposition use?
- How committed will the defence be?

Coaches have to make sure the whole team is involved. They should want every player to contribute 100 per cent. They must also plan strategies and tactics that take advantage of the actual strengths of the team. One player may have exceptional speed. Another may be able to kick long clearing distances with their left foot. The coach must take advantage of these talents in the

All Blacks coach Graham Henry talks tactics with his team. A coach must be a good communicator.

attacking and defensive plans. When you join the energy resources of the players to a realistic plan, success will come.

ENJOYMENT

A team should express itself to the fullest extent of its ability, play to the team plan and have fun. Rugby is an exciting and thrilling game. Learn and practise how to play it properly and enjoy!

The ultimate enjoyment is in achieving what you set out to do: South Africa, the World Champions.

LAWS OF THE GAME

Rugby is a simple game, but the laws are not. There are 22 major laws in rugby, and what follows is a simplified version. These are the current laws as the book goes to press, but new laws might have come into force since. If there is any dispute or you wish to be totally clear on a law, refer to the International Rugby Board for the full laws at www.irb.com. The websites for rugby unions in individual countries also include information on laws and regulations. The governing body of a particular union may also modify some of the laws to suit local and age-group competitions.

OBJECT

During a rugby match, two teams of 15 players try to score points by carrying, passing, kicking and grounding the ball. The object of the game is to be the team who scores the most points — the winner of the match. However, teams should play according to the laws and with a sporting spirit.

KEY POINTS FROM THE LAWS

- Any player on a rugby field can do anything (except that only front row players can play in the front row).
- Rugby is a game played on the feet.
- The senior law in rugby is "advantage", in order to keep the came continuous.
- The ball cannot be passed or thrown forward.
- A ruck consists of at least one player from each team in physical contact with the ball on the ground.
- A maul consists of at least three players on their feet with the ball held in the hands.

LAW 1: THE GROUND

The diagram opposite shows the size and markings of a rugby field.

DEFINITIONS

The playing area is everything on the diagram except the outside lines. When the ball or a player

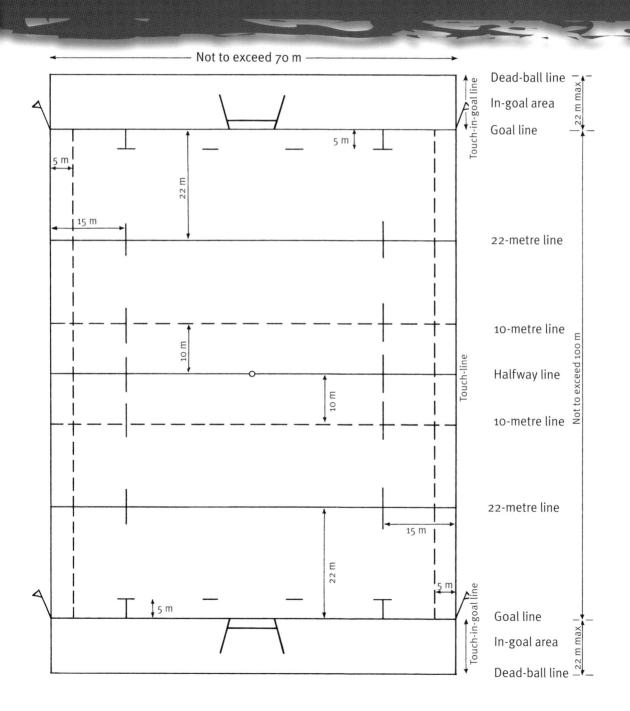

Not to exceed 70 m

Dead-ball line

In-goal area

Goal line

22 m max

Touch-in-goal line

5 m

22 m

15 m

5 m

22-metre line

10 m

10-metre line

Halfway line

Touch-line

10 m

10-metre line

Not to exceed 100 m

22-metre line

15 m

22 m

5 m

5 m

Goal line

Touch-in-goal line

In-goal area

22 m max

Dead-ball line

carrying it touches the outside lines it is out of play or "out" or, more commonly, "in touch".

The field of play is the area between the goal lines and the touch-lines but not the actual lines.

The in-goal area is between the goal line and the dead-ball line. It does include the goal line but does not include the dead-ball line.

IS THE BALL IN OR OUT?

- Ball or ball carrier touches a touch-line: out.
- Ball or ball carrier touches a corner flag: out.
- Ball or ball carrier touches touch-in-goal line (see diagram page 141): out.
- Ball or ball carrier touches a dead-ball line: out.
- Ball grounded by attacker on goal line or posts: try.
- Ball grounded by defender on goal line or posts: touch down.

SURFACE

The normal play surface is grass, but rugby may also be played on sand, clay, snow or artificial grass, as long as it is a safe surface.

DIMENSIONS

- **Field of play:** maximum 100 metres (about 109 yards) long and 70 metres (76½ yards) wide.

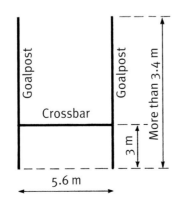

- **In-goal area:** maximum 22 metres (24 yards) long, but not less than 10 metres (11 yards).
- **Distance between goalposts:** 5.6 metres (about 6 yards).
- **Top edge of crossbar:** placed 3 metres (3¼ yards) above the ground.
- **Minimum height of goalposts:** 3.4 metres (3¾ yards).

OBJECTIONS

If either team is not satisfied with the ground, they should tell the referee before the match starts.

LAW 2: THE BALL

The ball must be oval, 280–300 millimetres (11–11 3/4 inches) long and 580–620 millimetres (22½–24 3/4 inches) in circumference at its widest, around the middle. The end-to-end, lengthwise circumference must be 740–770 millimetres. Balls of different sizes may be used for youth rugby.

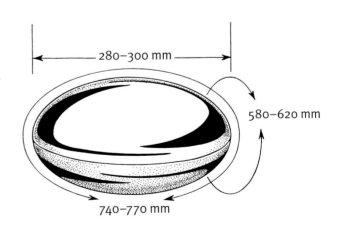

LAW 3: NUMBER OF PLAYERS

Each team has 15 players. Matches can take place with less than 15 players by agreement, but there must be at least five in the scrum. If a team has more than 15 players, the referee orders the extra player off and gives a penalty to the opposing team. Seven-a-side games have seven players per team.

DEFINITIONS

- **Replacement:** A player who replaces a teammate who is injured.
- **Substitute:** A player who replaces a teammate for tactical purposes.

CHANGING PLAYERS

There are seven replacements or substitutes in international matches. For other matches the parent union can nominate the number.

- A team can substitute up to two front row players and up to five other players.
- A referee can order an injured player off to be replaced or medically examined.
- A player ordered to the blood bin (where a player is sent when they have an injury and are bleeding) can be temporarily replaced (this is called a blood substitution).
- A player who is substituted cannot return to the match even to replace an injured player (except to replace a player in the blood bin or a front row forward, if the substituted player is a front row forward).

- If there are not enough front row forwards because they have been sent off or injured, scrums are uncontested. Neither team pushes and the team throwing in the ball wins it.

LAW 4: PLAYERS' CLOTHING

Players wear a jersey, shorts, underwear, socks and rugby shoes. They may also wear supports made of elasticized or compressible materials, shoulder pads, shin guards, ankle supports, fingerless gloves, a mouthguard, bandages and approved headgear. Women may also wear approved chest pads. Some unions make mouthguards compulsory for junior rugby.

A player cannot wear jewellery or anything hard, full gloves (although they can wear short catching gloves), shorts with padding sewn into them, or communication devices. The referee or the touch judge must inspect the players' clothing and shoe studs before a match.

LAW 5: TIME

A match lasts 80 minutes of actual play. It is divided into two halves of 40 minutes with a break in the middle of no more than 10 minutes. When time is up, the referee must end the match the next time the ball goes dead. But if the ref awards a mark, free kick, penalty kick or a conversion, then that play will also take place. In a knockout competition, extra time might be played if the match is tied at the end.

LAW 6: MATCH OFFICIALS

If there is no referee, the two teams appoint one. The home team appoints one if they cannot agree. During the match, the referee is the sole judge of the laws. The ref consults with the two touch judges, any timekeeper and the video ref (if there is one). Assistant referees are able to assist referees in any way the referee requires.

THE COIN TOSS

The referee organizes the toss before the match. One of the captains tosses a coin and the other one calls it. The winner either chooses the end they wish to play from, or to kick off. Whichever the winning captain chooses, the losing captain gets the other option.

THE TOUCH JUDGES

Unless appointed, each touch judge comes from one of the teams. The touch judges signal with a flag, which is raised to show the ball has gone out or a conversion has been successful. The flag is held to the chest to indicate foul play.

LAW 7: MODE OF PLAY

KICKOFF

The match is started by a kickoff. After that, any player can do anything that's within the laws. The only exception is that, for safety reasons, only front row players can play in the front row.

LAW 8: ADVANTAGE

If one team breaks the laws but the other team gains an advantage, the referee can allow them that advantage and keep play going. The length of time of the advantage is at the referee's discretion. The law of advantage is the most important law in terms of keeping play continuous. However, the referee cannot play advantage when there is a collapsed scrum or if a player in the scrum is lifted into the air.

LAW 9: METHODS OF SCORING

Try: an attacking player is the first to ground the ball in the opponent's in-goal area.

Penalty try: a try awarded when a player would probably have scored if not prevented by the foul play of an opponent. The conversion for a penalty try is taken in front of the posts.

Conversion: a kick at goal awarded after the scoring of a try. It is taken at a point in line with where the try was scored. It can be a place kick or a drop kick.

Penalty goal: a kick at goal after a penalty has been awarded.

Drop goal: a goal scored from a drop kick. A drop goal cannot be scored directly from a free kick. The ball must first go dead or be touched by an opponent or the ball carrier must be tackled.

POINTS' VALUES

- **Try:** 5 points
- **Penalty try:** 5 points

- **Conversion:** 2 points
- **Penalty goal:** 3 points
- **Drop goal:** 3 points

CONVERSIONS

Kickers have one minute to take the kick, starting from the time they place the ball. They can make a mark in the ground, use a kicking tee or sand. Even if the ball falls over in the wind, they still only have one minute. They can use a teammate as a placer to steady the ball. Except for the placer, all the kicker's team must be behind the ball when it is kicked.

The defending team must go behind the goal line and are not allowed to charge until the kicker starts to run. The kicker and the placer are not allowed to do any trick that makes the opposition charge early. If the ball falls over after the kicker has started to run up, the kicker can pick up the ball and drop kick it. The defending team can charge at this point. They are allowed to jump, but they are not allowed to support each other to stop the ball from crossing the crossbar.

LAW 10: FOUL PLAY

A player must play in the true spirit of the game and not do anything that may be considered bad sportsmanship.

DEFINITIONS

Foul play: anything a player does deliberately that is against the laws or the spirit of the game.
Unfair play: anything a player does unintentionally that is against the laws or the spirit of the game.
Penalty: allows a team to kick for goal, take a tap penalty or a kick into touch. Kicking the ball to touch allows them to have the throw-in to the line out.
Free kick: allows a team a free kick of the ball, but

they cannot kick directly at the goal, and if they kick the ball out, they will not get the throw-in.
Tap penalty: a penalty taken quickly in which the kicker kicks the ball forward a very short distance, usually into their own hands, and then runs forward with it.
Sin bin: a player who breaks the laws is sent off the field for 10 minutes.
Sending off: a player who breaks the laws is sent off the field for the rest of the match.

DANGEROUS PLAY

Striking: it is forbidden to punch, strike, kick, stamp, trample or trip an opponent, or to retaliate (strike an opponent because they have broken the law).

Tackling dangerously is forbidden. Dangerous tackles include:

- high tackle — above the shoulders;
- no arms tackle — without using the arms;
- spear tackle — throwing the player on to the head or shoulders;
- in the air — when a player's feet are off the ground, as in jumping to catch the ball;
- without the ball — such as a late charge on a kicker.

SCRUM

The front row of the scrum cannot:

- rush against its opponents;
- lift its opponents off their feet or force them up;
- collapse a scrum.

RUCK OR MAUL

Players must not:

- join a ruck or maul without binding on;
- collapse a ruck or maul.

Flying wedge: a team must not form a flying wedge, which is a group of players in formation, with or without the ball, charging at the opposition.

Cavalry charge: a team must not form a cavalry charge, which is a group of players charging on to a tap penalty.

OBSTRUCTION

Players are not allowed to obstruct opponents. Obstruction occurs in open play, when a player who does not have the ball blocks an opposing player and prevents them from getting to it. No player can push an opponent when chasing them for the ball (but they can push shoulder to shoulder).

THROWING THE BALL OFF THE FIELD OF PLAY

Players cannot deliberately throw or force the ball off the field with their arm or hand. However, they are allowed to kick the ball off the field.

PENALTY AWARDED AFTER A KICK

If a penalty is awarded to a team after they have taken a kick, it is awarded where the ball lands (although it must be at least 15 metres, or 16$\frac{1}{2}$ yards, in from the touch-line).

SIN BIN AND SEND-OFF

A player who commits an offence can be:

- cautioned (given a warning) by the referee;
- sin binned (a yellow card);
- sent off (a red card).

Repeated offences by several members of a team can result in the referee giving that team a general warning; if players offend further, the ref can send a player or players to the sin bin.

LAW 11: OFFSIDE AND ONSIDE IN GENERAL PLAY

OFFSIDE IN GENERAL PLAY

Offside generally means being in front of your own player who has the ball or in front of your own player who last played the ball (as in a kick).

Players will not normally be penalized when they are in an offside position unless they interfere with play or move towards the ball. However, they can be penalized for loitering (being offside and not getting out of the way) if they are preventing the opposing team from playing the ball.

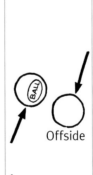

1
Offside player runs behind ball carrier

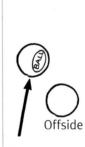

2
Teammate with ball runs ahead

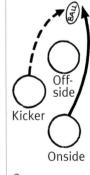

3
Teammate kicks, runs ahead or another onside teammate runs ahead

GETTING BACK ONSIDE

There are several ways in which an offside player can quickly get onside, as shown in the diagrams below and on the previous page.

- The offside player can run behind the ball carrier (1).
- The ball carrier can run in front of the offside player (2).
- The kicker can run in front of the offside teammate, or a teammate who is level with or behind the kicker can run in front of the offside player (3).
- An opponent who is carrying the ball may run 5 metres (5½ yards) (4).
- An opponent may kick or pass the ball (5).
- An opponent may intentionally touch the ball but not catch it (6).

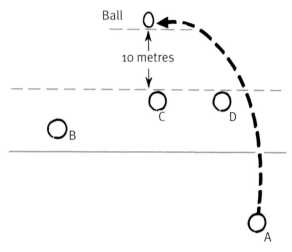

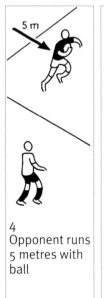
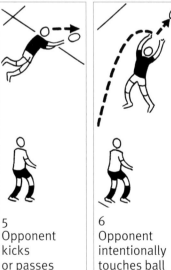

4
Opponent runs 5 metres with ball

5
Opponent kicks or passes

6
Opponent intentionally touches ball

THE OFFSIDE UNDER THE 10-METRE LAW

When a player (A in the diagram above) kicks the ball upfield, any teammate in front of them (B, C and D) must be at least 10 metres (11 yards) back from where the ball lands. If they are within 10 metres, they must retire to this imaginary line or they will be offside. However, they can be put onside if a teammate who started running from an onside position draws level with them. The 10-metre law does not apply when an offside player gets the ball from a charge down.

ACCIDENTAL OFFSIDE

When players in an offside position are touched by the ball or a teammate carrying the ball they are accidentally offside. A scrum is awarded to the opposing team.

OFFSIDE AFTER A KNOCK-ON

If a player knocks-on and a teammate who is in an offside position picks up the ball, a penalty is awarded to the opposing team.

LAW 12:KNOCK-ON OR THROW FORWARD

DEFINITIONS

Knock-on: called by the referee when a player loses the ball forward from the hand or arm and the ball touches another player or the ground before the first player can catch it.
Forward: moving towards the opposing team's dead-ball line.
Forward pass: when a player passes the ball forward to a teammate.
Charge down: when a player blocks a kick from the opposition with their body. Even if the ball strikes their arm or hand and goes forward, it is not a knock-on.

If the knock-on or forward pass is unintentional, the opponents are awarded a scrum; if it is intentional, they are awarded a penalty.

LAW 13: KICKOFF AND RESTART KICKS

KICKOFF

A kickoff is taken with a drop kick at or behind the centre of the halfway line. A restart kick is taken by the opponents of the team who scored.

- All of the kicker's team must be behind the ball when it is kicked.
- All the opposing team must stand on or behind their 10-metre line.
- The ball must reach the opponent's 10-metre

line or be played by an opponent first. If this does not happen, the opposing team has a choice between having a scrum at the centre or having the ball kicked again.

- If the ball goes out directly from a kickoff, the opposing team can have the ball kicked off again, a scrum at the centre or a throw-in where the ball went into touch.
- If the ball is kicked directly into the opposition's in-goal area, the defending team can touch it down immediately and then choose to have either a scrum at the centre or the kick retaken.

DROPOUT

A 22-metre (24-yard) dropout must be taken without delay.

- The opposing team cannot cross the 22-metre line before the ball is kicked.
- The ball must cross the 22-metre line, or the opposing team has a choice of another dropout or a scrum at the centre of the 22-metre line.
- If the dropout is kicked directly into touch, the opposing team can choose another dropout or a line out on the 22-metre line.

LAW 14: BALL ON THE GROUND — NO TACKLE

Rugby is played on the feet. When a player on the ground has the ball, they must immediately either:

- get up with the ball, or

- pass or release the ball (and move away from it immediately).

A player must not make the ball unplayable by falling down on it, lying on it or around it, or falling over other players who are on or near the ball.

LAW 15: TACKLE — BALL CARRIER BROUGHT TO THE GROUND

A tackle is made when the ball carrier is held by one or more opponents and is brought to ground. "Brought to ground" means the ball carrier has at least one knee on the ground or is sitting on the ground.

TACKLER

- Once the tackle is completed, tacklers must immediately release the tackled player and get up or move away from the tackled player.
- Tacklers must get to their feet before playing the ball.

TACKLED PLAYER

- Tackled players must try to make the ball available so play can continue.
- They must immediately release the ball.
- They can place the ball on the ground in any direction as long as they do it immediately.
- They can also push the ball as long as it is not pushed forward.

OTHER PLAYERS

- Opposition players who are on their feet can attempt to play the ball as long as they approach on their own side, from directly behind the tackle.

SCORING IN THE TACKLE

If a tackled player's momentum carries them into the in-goal area, they can score a try or make a touch down. If tackled short of the goal line, they can reach out and ground the ball as long as they do so immediately.

BALL UNPLAYABLE

If the ball becomes unplayable the referee must order a scrum immediately.

- The put-in is awarded to the team that was going forward.
- If no team was going forward, the put-in is awarded to the attacking team.

LAW 16: RUCK

FORMING A RUCK

For a ruck to form, at least one player must be in physical contact with an opponent, with both players on their feet and the ball on the ground. New players joining a ruck must:

- enter from the back;
- be on their feet;
- bind on to the ruck with at least the whole of one arm around the body of a teammate;
- make sure their heads and shoulders are no lower than their hips.

RESTRICTIONS AT A RUCK

- Jumping on a ruck is not permitted.
- Trying to collapse a ruck is not permitted.
- Players cannot be rucked when lying on the ground.
- The ball cannot be handled (played) with the hands, only the feet.
- Once the ball has left a ruck, it cannot be pulled back into it.

OFFSIDE AT THE RUCK

The players not in the ruck should be behind the feet of their rearmost teammates who are in the ruck.

ENDING A RUCK

A ruck ends when the ball comes out or is on or over the goal line. If the ball becomes unplayable, the referee awards a scrum to the team that was moving forward. If neither team was moving forward, then the scrum is awarded to the team that was moving forward before the ruck formed.

LAW 17: MAUL

FORMING A MAUL

A maul consists of at least three players on their feet. One is the ball carrier, one is the tackler and the third binds on to either of them. The offside laws for joining and binding to a maul are the same as those for a ruck. Also, a player must not try to drag an opponent out of a maul.

ENDING A MAUL

A maul ends when the ball or a player with the ball leaves the maul, when the ball is on the ground (in which case it becomes a ruck) or when the maul is over the goal line.

REFEREE ENDS MAUL

- If a maul collapses, remains stationary or has stopped moving forward for longer than five seconds, the referee ends it and awards a scrum to the team not in possession when the maul began (per the "use it or lose it" rule).
- If the ref is not sure who had possession, the scrum is awarded to the team moving forward before the maul stopped.
- If the maul was completely stationary, the attacking team gets the scrum.

MAUL VARIATIONS

- A maul that has stopped moving forward can start moving forward again if it does so within five seconds.
- If the maul has stopped moving forward for more than five seconds but the ball is moving, the ref can allow extra time for the team in possession to release the ball.
- If the ball carrier in a maul goes to ground (at least one knee or sitting), the ref orders a scrum unless the ball is released immediately.
- When a maul forms after a player catches the ball directly from an opposition punt, the scrum goes to the defending team.

LAW 18: MARK

CALLING A MARK

When the attacking team kicks the ball and a defender catches it behind the team's own 22-metre line (including their in-goal area) and shouts "mark", the ref will award a free kick.

- This stops opposing players from tackling the player who has called the mark.

- The catcher only needs one foot on the 22-metre line to call a mark.

- A mark cannot be made from a kickoff or a restart kick except for a dropout.

- The mark can be called even when the ball has first touched a goalpost or the crossbar.

TAKING A MARK

- The mark allows the player who caught the ball to take a free kick.

- The kick is taken from where the ball was caught.

- The opposition must not charge the kicker.

- If the ball is kicked directly to touch, the opposition will get the throw-in.

- If the player who took the mark is not a good kicker, they can kick the mark to themselves (tap the ball on their foot, as in a tap penalty) and then pass it to another player who kicks the ball.

- The player who took the mark is also allowed to tap the ball to themselves and then run with it.

- Rather than take a kick, the team awarded the mark has the option of taking a scrum.

LAW 19: TOUCH AND LINE OUT

DEFINITIONS

In touch: when the ball leaves the playing field.
Directly into touch: when the ball goes right out, without touching the ground or a player.
Indirectly into touch: when the ball hits a player or the ground before going out.

WHEN IS THE BALL IN TOUCH?

The ball is in touch when:

- it touches one of the field's outside lines or the corner flag;

- it crosses one of the outside lines and is not immediately brought back into play by a player (see below);

- a player in contact with the ball touches any body part against the outside lines, the ground off the field or the corner flag.

WHEN IS THE BALL NOT IN TOUCH?

The ball is still in play when:

- a player catches the ball over the touch-line while their feet are still in play;

- a player catches the ball in the air and both feet land in the playing area.

A player in touch can also knock the ball back into play, as long as it has not crossed the touch-line, but they must *knock* it backwards, not catch or hold it.

WHO GETS THE THROW-IN?

Generally, the throw-in is taken where the ball went into touch, but it must be at least 5 metres (5 1/2 yards) away from the goal line. It is usually taken by an opponent of the player who last held or touched the ball before it went out. When there is doubt, the attacking team takes the throw-in.

- When players kick the ball directly into touch from a penalty, their team gets the throw-in at the point where the ball went into touch.

- When players kick the ball directly into touch from inside their own 22-metre line, the opposing team gets the throw-in from where the ball went into touch.

- When players kick the ball directly into touch from outside their own 22, the opposing team gets the throw-in at a point level with where the ball was kicked (or where it went out if it was kicked backwards).

- If players get the ball outside their 22 and put it back inside their 22, then subsequently kick the ball directly into touch, the opposing team gets the throw-in at a point level with where the kick was made.

- When players kick indirectly into touch, the throw-in is taken where the ball went out.

QUICK THROW-IN

The team that has the right to the throw-in can take it without waiting for a line out to form — this is called a quick throw-in.

- The player who takes the quick throw-in must be the only player in the team to have touched the ball.

- The throw can be taken anywhere off the field between where the ball went into touch and the thrower's own goal line.

- The thrower has to use the ball that went into touch.

- The thrower can throw the ball in straight or towards the throwing team's goal line providing it crosses the 5 metre (5 1/2 yard) line.

- The thrower cannot take a quick throw-in once the line out has formed.

- Opposition players must not try to prevent a quick throw-in (though they can compete for the ball when it is in the field of play).

- If the ball carrier is forced into touch, they must release the ball to an opposition player so the opposition player has the opportunity to take a quick throw-in.

FORMING A LINE OUT

The number of players in the line out is determined by the team throwing in, but there must be at least two players from each team.

- Both teams form parallel lines at right angles to the touch-line with a metre (just under a yard) between them.

- Players not taking part in the line out must be back 10 metres (11 yards).

- The front of the line out must not be less than 5 metres (5 1/2 yards) from the touch-line and the back no more than 15 metres (16 1/2 yards) from the touch-line.

BEGINNING AND ENDING A LINE OUT

- The line out begins as soon as the ball leaves the hands of the player throwing it in.

- The line out ends when the ball or a player carrying it leaves the line out.

- No player from either team can leave the line out until it has ended.

- If the line out develops into a ruck or maul, then the offside line becomes the rearmost set of feet. However, the other players must remain

10 metres (11 yards) back until the line out has ended. Players who are in the line out must either join the ruck or maul or retire 10 metres.

LINE-OUT LAWS

- A line-out player must not hold, shove or jump off an opponent.

- The receiver at the line out (usually the scrum half) must be 2 metres ($2^{1}/_4$ yards) back, away from the line out.

- The player in opposition to the thrower must stand in the area between the 5-metre ($5^{1}/_2$-yard) line and touch line, and be 2 metres ($2^{1}/_4$ yards) from the line of touch and at least 2 metres from the line out.

- The lifting of line-out jumpers is permitted. Line-out players may pre-grip a jumper before the ball is thrown.

- The jumper must not use the outside arm on its own to catch or deflect the ball (but both arms or the inside arm can be used).

- Players are allowed to change their positions in the line out before the ball is thrown in.

LONG THROW-IN

If the ball is thrown beyond the 15-metre line (15 metres is about $16^{1}/_2$ yards), a teammate may run forward to catch it, which in turn allows an opponent to also run forward.

PEELING OFF

Peeling off is when a player leaves the line out to catch the ball knocked or passed back by a teammate.

- A player may peel off the line out when the ball has left the hands of the thrower.

- The player peeling off must keep moving until the line out has ended.

LAW 20: SCRUM

The scrum takes place where the infringement (a minor break of a law) occurred but not within 5 metres ($5^{1}/_2$ yards) of a touch-line or a goal line. A scrum usually has eight players and should not have less than five (see diagram overleaf). The team that did not cause the infringement puts the ball into the scrum.

FORMING A SCRUM

- Refs mark with their foot where the scrum is to be formed.

- The two scrums stand about an arm's length apart.

- The ball is in the scrum half's hands, ready to be thrown in.

- The referee calls "crouch" and the front rows crouch.

- The referee calls "touch" and, using their outside arm, each prop touches the opposing prop's outside shoulder.

- The props withdraw their arms.

- The referee calls "pause".

- There is a brief pause and then the referee calls "engage". This is not a command, but it tells the front rows they can now engage.

- The front rows come together with their heads and shoulders no lower than their hips and their heads interlocking so that no player's head is next to the head of a teammate.

- The scrum must remain stationary and level until the ball has left the scrum half's hands.

- No team can shove until the ball has been put in.

- The hooker's feet must be level until the ball is put in.

Positions of the forward packs in a typical scrum consisting of eight players from each team, and the scrum halves (9).

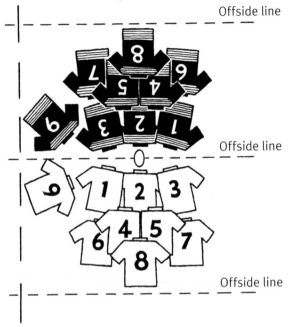

BINDING

- All of the front row forwards must bind firmly and continuously until the scrum ends.
- The whole arm, from hand to shoulder, must be used in binding.
- No player other than a prop may hold an opponent.
- Flankers must not widen the angle of their binding to obstruct the opposing scrum half moving forward.

LOOSEHEAD PROP BINDING

- The loosehead prop must bind on the opposing tighthead prop by putting the left arm inside the right arm of the tighthead and gripping the back or side of the tighthead prop's jersey.
- The loosehead prop must not grip the chest, arm, sleeve or collar of the opposition tighthead prop.

- The loosehead prop must not exert any downward pressure.

TIGHTHEAD PROP BINDING

- A tighthead prop must bind on to the opposing loosehead prop by placing the right arm outside the left upper arm of the opposing loosehead prop.
- The tighthead prop must grip the back or side of the loosehead prop's jersey with the right hand only.
- The tighthead prop must not grip the chest, arm, sleeve or collar of the opposition loosehead prop.
- The tighthead prop must not exert any downward pressure.

PUTTING THE BALL INTO THE SCRUM

The scrum half puts the ball into the scrum when told to with one forward movement (no backwards movement is permitted). The scrum half uses both hands to throw the ball along the middle line of the scrum.

- The ball should go in about midway between the knees and ankles of the players in the scrum, hitting the ground just beyond the nearest prop's shoulders.
- The scrum half cannot pretend to throw the ball in.
- If the scrum half throws the ball in and it comes out of the tunnel, the ball must be thrown in again.
- Once the ball touches the ground in the tunnel, any front row player can use either foot to try to win possession of the ball, but no player is allowed to raise both feet at the same time.

SCRUM COLLAPSE AND LIFTING

- Front row players must not twist or lower their bodies, pull opponents or do anything that is likely to collapse the scrum, either when the ball is being thrown in or afterward.
- If a scrum collapses, the referee must blow the whistle immediately to stop players pushing.
- If a player in a scrum is lifted or forced up out of the scrum, the referee must blow the whistle immediately to stop the other players pushing.

OFFENCES

- Players cannot handle the ball in the scrum or fall on the ball.
- The ball cannot be brought back into the scrum.
- A scrum half cannot kick the ball while it is in the scrum.
- The scrum half cannot do anything to make the opponents think that the ball is out of the scrum while it is still in the scrum.
- The scrum half cannot hold an opposing flanker.

ENDING THE SCRUM

The scrum ends when:

- the ball comes out (except for when it comes straight out the tunnel);
- the ball is on or over the goal line and may be grounded by either an attacker or defender;
- the ball is at the number eight's feet, and the number eight unbinds to pick up the ball.

WHEELING OF THE SCRUM

If a scrum is wheeled through more than 90 degrees, a new scrum is set with the ball put in by the team that was not in possession when play was stopped.

OFFSIDE AT THE SCRUM

In order for players to be onside:

- the scrum half not throwing the ball must stand either next to the scrum half who is throwing in the ball or behind the feet of the rearmost player in the scrum;
- when the ball is in the scrum, the scrum half who put it in must have at least one foot behind the ball;
- the defending scrum half must have both feet behind the ball;
- the offside line is 5 metres ($5^1/_2$ yards) behind the hindmost feet of the scrum, except for the opposing scrum half.

LAW 21: PENALTY AND FREE KICKS

Penalty kicks are taken at the mark indicated by the referee (usually where the infringement occurred). The ball can be kicked with any part of the lower leg (but not the knee or heel). A team awarded a penalty or free kick can choose to get the put-in at a scrum instead.

- A player cannot place the ball on the ground and kick for touch.
- Once the ball is kicked, the kicker can play it again before anyone else has touched it.
- All of the kicker's team must be behind the ball (except the placer for a place kick).
- If a penalty or free kick is taken quickly with teammates in front of the kicker, they are not offside if they retire immediately.
- Offside players become onside when the kicker or

other teammates who were behind them run level with the previously offside players.

SCORING A GOAL FROM A PENALTY KICK

- Once kickers tell the referee they intend to kick at goal, they must kick at goal. The kicker can place the ball directly on the ground, on sand, sawdust or a kicking tee.
- While kickers make their approach, the opposing team must stand still with their hands by their sides until the ball is kicked.

SCORING FROM A FREE KICK

- A goal cannot be scored from a free kick.
- A team cannot score a drop goal after a free kick until the ball has become dead, or an opponent has played or touched it or tackled the ball carrier.
- This rule also applies if the team chooses a scrum instead of a free kick.

OPPOSING TEAM AT A PENALTY KICK

- The opposing team must retreat 10 metres (11 yards) or to their goal line if that is closer.
- Even if the attacking team takes a tap penalty, players of the opposing team must retreat 10 metres before they can take part in the game again.
- The opposition must not throw the ball away to prevent a tap penalty or try to stop the kicker from taking a tap penalty.
- Once the opposing players have retreated 10 metres, they can try to charge the ball as soon as the kicker approaches to take the kick.
- The kicker cannot pretend to kick.

LAW 22: IN-GOAL

GROUNDING THE BALL

A player can ground the ball in the in-goal by touching it to the ground or pressing it down to the ground (downward pressure) with one or both hands, one or both arms, or the front of the body from waist to neck.

- A try is scored if attacking players are the first to ground the ball in their opponent's in-goal.
- It is a touch down if the defending players are first to ground the ball in their own in-goal.
- Picking up the ball from the ground in the in-goal is not grounding it. A player may, however, pick up the ball and ground it elsewhere in the in-goal.

OTHER WAYS TO SCORE A TRY

Goal line: if the ball is grounded on the goal line by an attacker, it is a try.

Goalposts: if the ball is grounded by an attacking player against a goalpost or the padding around them, it is a try.

Push-over try: if a scrum, ruck or maul crosses the goal line and the ball is grounded by an attacker, it is a try.

Momentum try: if an attacker is tackled short of the goal line but momentum carries the player forward in a continuous movement along the ground and the attacker is able to ground the ball, it is a try.

Reaching out: in the same way, a player who is tackled short of the goal line can reach out and score a try.

In the last two situations, defenders on their feet can try to prevent the try by wrestling the ball free, but they are not allowed to kick it.

RESTARTING AFTER A TOUCH DOWN

- A drop-out is awarded to the defending team if an attacker sends or carries the ball into the opponent's in-goal and the ball is grounded by a defender or goes out of play.
- If the ball is immediately touched down or goes dead in the defender's in-goal directly from a kickoff, the defenders choose between retaking the kickoff or a scrum at the centre.
- A scrum at the 5-metre line, called a 5-metre scrum (5 metres is around 5 ½ yards), is awarded to the attacking team if a defending player takes the ball into the in-goal and grounds it.

BALL KICKED DEAD IN IN-GOAL

If a team kicks the ball so that it goes out of play in the opponent's in-goal, the defending team can choose to have a dropout or a scrum from where the ball was kicked. This does not apply if the attacking team is taking a penalty kick.

BALL HELD UP IN IN-GOAL

A 5-metre scrum is awarded to the attacking team if an attacking player carries the ball into the in-goal but cannot ground it.

BALL DEAD IN IN-GOAL

The corner posts are not considered to be touch in-goal, except when the ball is grounded against the post.

DOUBT ABOUT GROUNDING

If there is doubt about who grounded the ball, play is restarted with a 5-metre scrum awarded to the attacking team.

GLOSSARY

10-metre line — the line either side of the halfway line past which the ball has to be kicked at a kickoff.

22-metre dropout — a drop kick to restart play that is taken by the defending team from behind their 22-metre line (22 metres is around 24 yards).

22-metre line — the line on the field of play that marks a team's defensive zone (also called the 22).

Advantage — when the referee allows play to continue because the non-offending team has possession of the ball and they have gained a clear advantage.

Against the head — winning the ball at the scrum when the other team has put it in.

American football pass — a long one-handed overhead pass across the field (similar to a quarterback pass in American football).

Ankle tap — striking the ball carrier's ankle from behind, causing a loss of balance.

"Anything goes" pass — any pass, no matter how awkward, that reaches the receiver.

Back line — the line of backs waiting to defend or attack.

Backs — the players who stand behind the scrum (*see also* Forwards and Backs, page 15).

Back row — the three outside (loose) players in the scrum.

Back three — the fullback and the two wings.

Ball carrier — the person carrying the ball.

Binding — holding on to another player with the full arm.

Blind side — the space between the ball and the nearest touch-line (compare open side).

Blind-side charge — an attacking move on the blind side of the field.

Blind-side defence — defence on the blind side of the field.

Bobbing ball — the ball bouncing along the ground unevenly.

Body position — the alignment of the whole body when carrying out a technique.

Box kick — a high kick aimed so the ball lands in front of the opposing wing.

Breakdown — when possession of the ball has been temporarily halted and is being contested by both sides. A tackle is usually the point of breakdown.

Bump [off] — the ball carrier knocks back the tackler by bumping a shoulder against their shoulder.

Centre — playing position in the middle of the back line.

Change-of-direction pass — pretending to pass in one direction, then passing in the opposite direction instead.

Channel — a route between the players' legs taken by the ball when it is coming back through the scrum (there are three main channels).

Chip kick or **Chip-and-chase kick** — a short kick over an opponent's head.

Code — secret signals or messages a team uses to communicate planned moves.

Conversion — the kick at goal following a try.

Corner flag — the flags at the corners of the goal line and the touch-line.

Counterattack — an attacking move in response to an opposition attack after possession has changed hands.

Cross kick — a kick across the field towards the attacking team's open wing position.

Cut-back pass — a pass to a player who cuts back in the opposite direction (also called a scissors pass).

Cut-out pass — a pass that misses out a player in the attacking team and is intended for the next player out (also called a miss-pass).

Dart — a sudden movement in a different direction.

Dead-ball line — the line at each end of the field of play. When the ball or the player carrying the ball touches it, the ball is said to be "dead".

Decoy — a player who pretends to be about to get the ball to confuse the opposition.

Defence — the system, tactics or actions used to counter an opposition attack.

Delaying the pass — the ball carrier holding on to the ball longer than usual before passing to try to break up the rhythm of the defence.

Dive pass — passing the ball while diving towards the catcher.

Dodge — to move quickly to the side to avoid a tackler.

Drawing the player — committing an opponent to making the tackle before passing.

Drift defence — a system of defence that drifts sideways across the field.

Drive — to push forward by driving the legs hard against the ground.

Driving maul — a maul in which the opposition is driven back.

Driving tackle — when the tackler pushes the ball carrier backwards.

Drop goal — a drop kick from the field of play that sends the ball over the crossbar.

Drop kick — a kick that strikes the ball immediately after it has been deliberately dropped to the ground.

Dropout — a restart of play in which the defending team drop kicks from behind their own 22-metre line.

Drubber — a short, flat kick (also called a grubber kick).

Dummy or **Dummy pass** — a pretend pass.

Dummy kick — a pretend kick.

Engagement — when the opposing front rows of the scrum come together.

Extra time — time added on by the referee for injuries and stoppages.

Fair catch — a player catching the ball inside their own 22 when the opposition has kicked it (also called a mark).

Fast pass — when the ball is passed as soon as it is caught because the receiver is about to be tackled.

Feint — a fake move to deceive an opponent.

Fend — when the ball carrier uses the arm and open hand to push off an opponent (also called a hand-off).

Field of play — the whole of the playing field between the two dead-ball lines.

First five-eighth — the fly half.

Five-metre scrum — a scrum 5 metres (5 1/2 yards) from the defending team's goal line (*see also* page 157 under Law 22).

Flanker — one of the two players on either side, or flank, in the third, or back, row of the scrum (also called a wing forward).

Flick pass — a pass using a flick of the wrist.

Fly half — the back who stands between the scrum half and the inside centre.

Forward charge — an aggressive run by a forward with the ball in which the player tries to knock opponents out of the way.

Forward pass — when a player throws a pass towards the front. This is an illegal move in rugby.

Foul play — play that is dangerous or against the rules or the spirit of the game.

Free kick — a lesser grade of penalty that, when awarded, does not allow the kicker to take a direct kick at goal.

Front-on tackle — a tackle in which the ball carrier runs straight at the tackler.

Front row — the first row of forwards in the scrum, consisting of two props and a hooker.

Fullback — the player nearest to the team's own goalposts.

Full stop — to suddenly stop dead with the ball, usually done to confuse the opposition.

Full time — the end of the match.

Gain line — an imaginary line between the two teams that must be crossed for one team to gain a territorial advantage over the other.

Gang tackle — two or more opposing players tackling the ball carrier.

Garryowen — the up-and-under kick, named after an Irish club that used it frequently.

Goal — a successful kick between the goalposts.

Goal line — the line the goals are on (also called the try line).

Goalposts — the upright posts that make up the goal.

Goose step — a short step with the knees locked.

Grounding — forcing the ball against the ground in the in-goal area with the hands, arms or upper body.

Grubber — a short, flat kick (also called a drubber kick).

Gumshield — a plastic guard that is placed in the mouth over the upper row of teeth (also called a mouthguard).

Hack kick — a kick ahead of the loose ball.

Halfback — the back who stands closest to the scrum (also called the scrum half).

Halfback pass — a long pass from the forwards to the backs.

Half hold — when the ball carrier is held but not fully tackled.

Hand-off — when the ball carrier uses the arm and open hand to push off an opponent (also called a fend).

High tackle — a dangerous and illegal tackle above the line of the shoulders.

Hit and spin — a forward charge in which the ball carrier manages to spin out of the tackle.

Hooker — the player who hooks back the ball in the scrum.

Hospital pass — a poorly timed pass that reaches the catcher at the same time as the tackler (thus risking injury).

In-goal — the area of the field between the goalposts and the dead-ball line.

Infringement — breaking one of the rules for which the referee will award a penalty to the non-offending team.

Inside centre — centre closest to the scrum.

In touch — off the field of play.

Jump — to leap vertically off the ground, usually to catch the ball.

Kickoff — the start of a match or the restart after one team has scored.

Knock-on — when the ball has struck a player's hands or arms, gone forward then hit the ground or another player.

Line out — the players lined up to catch the ball when it is thrown back on to the field.

Line-out calls — the coded calls telling the jumpers of the team throwing in where the ball is going.

Lob pass — a pass over an opponent's head.

Lock — one of the two second row forwards in the middle of the scrum.

Long pass — a longer than normal pass across the field.

Loop — when a players runs around a teammate they have just passed to in order to receive the ball back again.

Loosehead prop — the prop on the left side of the team's own scrum.

Loosie — a common name for the three players of the back row of the scrum who are able to disengage more quickly than the tight five. They are the players expected to be first to the loose ball or breakdown.

Mark — 1. The place from which a penalty, free kick or scrum is taken. 2. A defender catching the ball from an opposition kick inside their own 22 (also called a fair catch).

Marking — watching and staying with an opponent, ready to tackle.

Maul — a wrestle for the ball between both teams.

Miss-out pass — a pass that misses out one attacking player and is meant for the next player in the line (also called a cut-out pass).

Mobile — being able to move rapidly around the field.

Mouthguard — a plastic guard that is placed in the mouth over the upper row of teeth (also called a gumshield).

Non-offending team — the team that has not broken a law (compare offending).

Non-pass — when the ball carrier changes speed or direction as if about to pass but doesn't pass and speeds up again.

Normal pass — the normal pass made by a running player using a swing of the arms and body to pass the ball to a teammate.

Number eight — the player at the back of the scrum.

Obstruction — illegally getting in the way of an opposition player.

Offending team — the team that has broken a law (compare non-offending).

Offside — when a player is standing where prohibited, usually in front of the ball (*see also* Law 11 on pages 146–147 for more information).

One-handed pass — passing the ball with one hand.

One-handed tap back — a line-out jumper knocking the ball back towards the team's own side with one hand.

Onside — being in a fair position, usually behind the ball.

Open play — when play is moving around the field without being stopped by the referee.

Open rugby — fast, flowing rugby.

Open side — the space between the ball and the farthest touch-line (compare blind side).

Out — off the field of play.

Outside centre — the centre who stands farthest from the team's own scrum.

Outside cut — a swerve towards the outside of the field.

Outside-in defence — when the defenders nearest the touch-line mark opposition players standing in from them.

Overhead pass — when a player lifts the ball above the head to get the pass over the head of a tackler.

Over-the-shoulder kick — a kick, often made by the scrum half, when facing the wrong way and under pressure from the opposition.

Over-the-top throw — a long throw that goes right over the top of the line out.

Overlap — when one side has an extra player on the outside.

Pass — when a player throws the ball to a teammate.

Passing on — when the ball is quickly passed out towards the wings.

Peel — a move in which a forward runs the ball up from the line out.

Penalty kick or Penalty — a free kick of the ball awarded to one team when the other team has broken the rules.

Penalty try — a try awarded by the referee when the attacking team would have scored but for foul play by the opposition.

Penetrator — an attacking player who breaks through the defence of the opposition.

Pick-and-go — a forward charge in which the ball is put on the ground in the tackle and the next forward picks it up and runs with it.

Pivot — a player who sets up a penetration move. Also another name for the fly half.

Place kick — kicking the ball after it is placed on the ground.

Player-on-player defence — a system of defence in which the tackler takes the player directly opposite.

Player-out defence — a system of defence in which the tacklers line up their players from the outside of the field inward.

Pop pass — a very short pass.

Positions — where the players stand on the field, which is fixed in set play.

Prop — the players in the scrum who support the hooker.

Punt — to kick the ball from the hand.

Push-over try — a try scored as a result of the attacking team pushing their opponent's scrum over their own goal line.

Quality ball — good, clean possession that can be used to create an attack.

Quick throw-in — a throw into the line out taken quickly before the line out has formed.

Referee — the official on the field who ensures both teams keep to the laws of the game.

Retire — to resume an onside position, either behind a teammate about to kick the ball or 10 metres (11 yards) from an opposing player about to take a free kick or penalty.

Reverse flick — a pass thrown backwards by the ball carrier to a teammate in behind.

Ripping the ball — pulling the ball free at a maul (also called stripping the ball).

Rolling maul — a maul in which the attacking team constantly changes the point of attack to the left or the right while going forward.

Ruck — when the ball is on the ground and both teams are trying to push each other off it.

Rules — the agreed laws on how the game will be played.

Scissors pass — passing to a player who cuts back in the opposite direction (also known as a cut-back pass).

Screw kick — a kick that causes the ball to spin through the air (also called a spiral kick).

Scrum or Scrummage — a set-piece pushing contest between two teams.

Scrum half — the player closest to the scrum (also called the halfback).

Scrum-half pass — a long pass by the scrum half to clear the ball from the forwards to the backs.

Scrum machine — a machine used at scrum practice for the forwards to practice pushing against. It can be made with weights attached to a homemade sled.

Second five-eighth — the inside centre.

Second phase — when both teams are contesting possession of the ball.

Second row — the two locks, who form the second row of forwards in the scrum.

Set piece or Set play — a set way of restarting play, such as a scrum or line out.

Shortened line out — when the team throwing in calls for less than seven players to take part in the line out.

Side-on tackle — a tackle made into the side of the ball carrier.

Side step — to evade a tackler by quickly stepping to one side before proceeding.

Sin bin — when a player must leave the field for 10 minutes for illegal play.

Smother tackle — a type of tackle in which the ball carrier's arms are held, or smothered, so the ball can't be passed.

Spin — the rotation of the ball as it is propelled through the air.

Spin pass — a pass that causes the ball to spin through the air (also called a spiral pass).

Spiral kick — a kick that causes the ball to spiral through the air (also called a screw kick).

Spiral pass — a pass that causes the ball to spiral through the air (also called a spin pass).

Stationary tackle — a tackle made when the ball carrier is running at a tackler who is standing still.

Stiff-arm tackle — a dangerous tackle made with the arms straight.

Stripping the ball — pulling the ball free at a maul (also called ripping the ball).

Swerve — to deviate from a straight line, usually at speed.

Support — to follow closely; to back up the ball carrier.

Tackle — to stop the ball carrier and (usually) take them to the ground.

Tackled-ball pass — a pass made by a ball carrier who has been tackled but still has one or both hands free.

Tactics — a way of working as a team to beat the opposition.

Tap kick or Tap penalty — a short penalty kick used when the attacking team intends to run with the ball.

Technique — the exact means of achieving one's purpose.

Three-quarter — the centres and wings.

Throw forward — when the ball is thrown, deliberately or accidentally, in the direction of the opposition goal line (not level or backwards). It is illegal and results in a penalty.

Tight five — the name given to the tightly bound front and second row forwards who do the hard, or tight, work in the scrums, line outs, rucks and mauls.

Tight forward — a forward in the front or second row who does most of the "heavy" work, such as at scrums, rucks and mauls.

Tighthead — hooking the ball in the scrum when the other team has put it in.

Tighthead prop — the prop on the right side of the team's own scrum, farthest away from where the scrum half puts the ball in.

Touch or Touch-line — the lines at the side of the field of play. When they are touched by the ball or the player carrying it, the ball is said to be out.

Touch judge — the official on the touch-line who signals when the ball is out.

Touch down — a defender grounding the ball in the team's own in-goal area.

Touch-line tackle — a tackle that pushes or drives the ball carrier over the touch-line.

Truck and trailer — a rolling maul where the team with the ball has separated into two groups: the forward group (without the ball) illegally protecting the second group, which has the ball.

Try — the grounding of the ball by an attacking player in the opponent's in-goal area.

Try line — the line on or beyond which a try is scored (also called the goal line).

Unit — a small group of players working together.

Upright — one of the posts that make up the goalposts.

Up-and-under — a high kick to test or put pressure on the opposition (also called a Garryowen).

Wheel — when a scrum moves through more than 90 degrees.

Willie-away — a peel from the line out, named after New Zealander Wilson Whineray (*see also* peel).

Wing or Wing three-quarter — the players closest to the touch-lines.

Wing forward — another name for a flanker.

Wipers kick — an angled kick across the field (with an angle similar to that of a windshield wiper).

INDEX